HINDSIGHT
TO
INSIGHT

Money Between Family & Friends

Sabrina Protic

Four Time *Bestselling Author*

PRAISE FOR *HINDSIGHT TO INSIGHT*

Hindsight to Insight explains how we inherit our money culture from our parents. If they're not financially savvy, we may continue to repeat money mistakes from one generation to the next, preventing us from achieving financial freedom. Author Sabrina Protic includes insightful anecdotes to illustrate why financial literacy is an essential part of our education. This short, easy-to-read book is valuable for anyone who wants more confidence and success around money.

C. J. Grace
Bestselling author of *Adulterer's Wife: How to Thrive Whether you Stay or Not,* **and the comic memoir,**
My Wild Ride: How to Thrive After Breast Cancer and Infidelity

I enjoyed the lessons Sabrina shared in this book. I could relate to her and her money stories, seeing some of them in myself. She is very relatable. Someone reading a book on Financial Status may want to overlook it thinking they are not in a financial situation to need to know how to manage or plan for their financial future, but this author manages to connect with the reader, making it all make sense.

Hindsight To Insight has opened my eyes to areas I had not considered in my "financial house." I will definitely be making some changes!

I would 100% recommend this book to friends, family, and clients. Sabrina breaks down the overwhelming topic of money into relatable and realistic terms. Anyone who reads this book will gain from it. This author is one of the smartest women I have met and her passion to help others radiates in everything she does.

Dara Bose
Author, NLP Practitioner, Speaker, Certified Life Coach

Hindsight to Insight is a fabulous introduction to understanding wealth, wealth building, and creating financial freedom. From the very start of this book, the author walks you through thinking about your own money journey. She encourages you to think about how your own perception and ideas about money development. She doesn't leave you there though. She walks you through the process of knowing what building and creating wealth in an easy-to-understand language. This book is for every person who wants to begin to build wealth but has no idea where to start. Sabrina holds your hand through the entire book! What a great read!

Sherri Leopold
WOW WARRIOR Founder,
Leader of the Stop Self-Bullying Movement

In *Hindsight to Insight*, Sabrina is able to talk about finances in an accessible way. If you are a real person, with a real struggle, and want to create wealth, Sabrina is the teacher you've been waiting for. She shares actionable steps you can take to start changing your life now. A must-read for anyone on their path to financial wellness and abundance.

Navi Bliss
Love and Confidence Coach

When you know better, you do better. That's why this book is an essential read for children as well as adults in order for them to become better stewards of their income. Sabrina Protic shares practical tips and strategies to navigate financial situations with grace and skill. She shares her relationships with money as she grew up from childhood to adulthood which will mirror many readers' stories when it comes to their knowledge and handling of money. This book is an easy read with practical information that anyone can use today and every day!

Sabrina Protic is a ray of sunshine. She uses her own stories of the challenges, trials, and triumphs on her road to financial freedom to help others see a path to their own financial freedom. She is knowledgeable, approachable, and has a genuine desire to help others reach the next level of their greatness.

Terrance "The UnStopABLE Coach" Leftridge

Publish@nowscpress.com
www.PublishWithNOW.com
@nowscpress

Ordering Information:

Quantity sales. Special discounts are available on quantity purchases by corporations, associations, and others. For details, contact the publisher at the address above.

Orders by U.S. trade bookstores and wholesalers. Please contact: NOW SC Press: Tel: (813) 970-8470 or visit www.PublishWithNOW.com

Printed in the United States of America

First Printing 2023

ISBN: 979-8-9870349-6-5

DEDICATION

This book is dedicated to my son and daughter and my entire lineage as an indelible legacy footprint of lessons and knowledge to guide them to a financially secure and happy life now and in the years to come. This dedication encompasses all international communities of people of all ages as a stepping stone to building and growing financially which fosters peace, love and happiness for all generations.

CONTENTS

SECTION III
THE FLOW OF MONEY

SECTION IV
WEALTH BUILDING

FOREWORD

Relationships. Relationships drive many of our decisions, experiences, and identity. Most of us can pinpoint the highs and lows of our lives to positive or negative relationships. Well, money is the same way. We are in a relationship with money.

I was on my own relationship journey with money, which started out with $100,000 worth of debt and I had no financial literacy to guide me. And boy was it a journey—a journey of making a decision, being truthful with my numbers, knowing I was worthy of my definition of success and dealing with external and internal forces that caused me to spend.

Wow!

Now, after paying all the debt off in 2015, I look back. When you stop and really take stock of just how important it is to understand the financial game being played all around you, it really makes you more aware of both sides of the playing field—the offensive and the defensive. There are no professional sports teams that just practice one side of the game. They don't just work on blocking. They don't just focus on shooting. They make sure their teams are strong on both ends.

Sabrina's stories, case studies, and examples help you gain expertise for both sides of the game.

The offense consists of the outer game tactics. This is the budgeting, planning, goal setting, and managing the net worth numbers. The defense focuses on training areas that aren't so easy to see. This includes your internal belief systems, advertising mind tricks, and how marketers can influence your identity to increase your consumption. To be successful in handling your finances, you need to address both sides. You need to draw up game plans for both tactics. Weakness on one end could mean disaster.

If you have your goals set and your plans laid out, even if life throws you a shock, you're better able to absorb it. If one of your best players gets injured, the other teammates are strong enough to compensate for that temporary loss. With the training you're learning with this book and other resources, you're ready for battle. You've got this!

After I figured out this was a game, I then learned how to play it. I learned how to develop my creative skills to create the life I want. This book reviews the plays needed to win the game of money and even in the game of life.

Now that I'm winning, I have realized, it's just like Monopoly. You get engrossed in the game, employ your strategies and make sure people don't take advantage of you. You invest and have people land on your property and pay you dividends and rent. If you think strategically, you can win the entire tournament! Yet, when the game is over, when all is said and done, the pieces all go back into the box.

After I asked myself this thought-provoking question, I knew I wanted to do more than just win this financial game. I desired to create a life of contribution with my money. My money needed a mission. My cash needed a cause. My provision needed a purpose. When you get your money on the right track, it can be used for a bigger purpose.

Sabrina's guidelines help you see that bigger purpose. **This is your life, and it is your money.**

Greatness can exude from both and take you from *Hindsight to Insight* if you take the time to learn, apply and contribute with joy.

Genein Letford, M.Ed

Award-winning educator and author of the best-selling book From *Debt to Destiny,* Creating Financial Freedom from the Inside Out

Money, Family, and Friends

MONEY CULTURE

Money Culture

View of Money as a Child

Saving Money Growing Up

Freedom to Discuss Money

LifeStyle

CHAPTER ONE

MONEY CULTURE

When you hear money, does something magically happen in your mind? Perhaps you become excited, nervous, afraid, empowered, depressed, scared, or even paranoid. This roller coaster of emotions could be due to our generational money culture. The word "generational" refers to our parents, grandparents, great-grandparents, and entire lineage. This inherited financial perspective could determine how we eat, sleep, drink, smell, think, and react to money.

For centuries people have been stereotyped by money. Perhaps you may have heard inferences such as "born with a silver spoon in your mouth," "born into poverty," "born into money," and "born rich and born poor." In my locale, some communities are referred to as "old money," meaning they are considered the affluent giants from my grandparents and great-grandparents' time. My dad used to take us for our weekly family Sunday drives through some of these sprawling estates. I remember my brother, sister, and I oohing and awing at the huge mansions with neatly manicured lawns as if they were so far out of our reality.

We are not alone in our mental processing as entire communities and countries conduct commerce due to how humans respond to money and the appearance of abundance or the lack thereof. These money traits are passed on from generation to generation. Some cultures teach their children to save money, while others teach their kids to be free with money and spend, spend, spend to enjoy life. What about money equality? In some cultures, males are offered higher salaries than women in the same job class and experience. Economically speaking, certain cultures and classes of people are perceived by some as having an abundance of money. Do we find ourselves adapting to these perceptions?

What is money? It is simply a currency that, in material form, can be coins, paper, EFTs, and cryptocurrency. Money is a monetary exchange for goods and services. I have often thought that each country can make money, so why not make enough currency for everyone in abundance? I had only seen boatloads of money when my spouse and I took our kids to the US Mint on vacation. It was a nice experience to see how money is made and what happens to defective coins and dollar bills. We purchased virgin money. This is money that human hands have never touched. This was over twenty-five years ago. Because I was a mature adult, I understood the value of preserving this investment and not spending it frivolously. Regrettably and ignorantly, I spent money my mother gave us as teenagers for safekeeping, such as the $2 bill, Kennedy 50-cent coins, and certain other currencies. I was desperate for money at the time and had not been taught its long-term value. I still lament over that to this day. Have you started a coin collection for your children? This would be a great start at teaching currency values and investments.

> Have you started a coin collection for your children?

Think briefly about your upbringing and what you were taught about money. Did your family discuss money at all? Were you allowed to touch money, and if so, at what age did this happen? Perhaps money was scarce, and this created a sense of anxiety when the subject was mentioned. Did your mom or dad entrust you with money? I recall my mother sending me to the corner store with 25 cents to purchase a 10-cent loaf of bread. I returned home with the loaf of bread and no change. My mother was furious, and I felt like she was angry with me. She yelled at me, making me feel like I had done something wrong. This created a fear of money early in my life and insecurity about handling it. The truth is that the store owner had cheated me due to my ignorance and had not given me the proper change back. I feared trusting people and was sure that everyone was a cheat. In my mind, you had to watch your back with your money in my community culture. The sad part about this story is that my mother knew the store owner. She drove me back to that store, took me inside, and demanded her change back. Of course, the store owner complied and pretended it was an error. Looking back, I needed lessons such as learning to count money and be accountable and comfortable with it.

Some cultures teach people to trust no one, and others teach them to trust everyone with money. Have you ever been to someone's home and seen money lying on the table with wallets and purses sitting out freely? Then there are other homes where, when you walk in, they secure their belongings. The woman will grab her purse and put it away. Why is this? It's the culture of money. This is a reaction to a belief that something will or will not happen with their valuables. There are some environments where I have left my purse completely unattended. There is a trust factor among certain friends and family members. I feel that my money is safe.

On the other hand, sometimes my purse does not leave my side and is securely attached to my hand, shoulder or body. What determines this caution? I had a bad habit of leaving my purse wide open at work where people could see my money and wallet. While sitting at my desk, my purse was visible for anyone nearby to catch a glimpse. There were plenty of times when I left my purse unattended to help a customer at the counter or go to the bathroom. A male co-worker approached me one day and told me to watch my purse. He said I was not being careful with my valuables. He knew something that I did not. People's views on money were vastly different, and I had a false sense of money safety.

> I had a false sense of money safety.

There's always that family member, friend, or iconic neighborhood figure with more money than anyone else. It can be a lure of attraction to want to be like that person, even in the case of ill-begotten gain. The flash of cash pardons the shadiness of the abundance of money. In my neighbor, one guy had all the trappings with the money to burn and all the assets to prove it. We knew the source of the money was not legal, but it seemed to come with the territory of where I lived. All the girls flaunted in front of him and wanted to be his girlfriend. Sadly, I lost a few classmates to ill-begotten gain because it was too easy to get in but hard to get out. My parents worked hard to keep us from idolizing this means of getting cash. They were proud that we did not succumb to the appearance of easy money. They taught us to work for our money. We became financially responsible by securing jobs for income when we were teens and old enough for employment.

The financial footprints we make can be determined by the experiences we have growing up. We are shaped by our environment but not indelibly. Many people made a 360-degree turn in life financially, from bad to good. Some have served time in prison and turned their lives around successfully and financially. An example is Frank William Abagnale, a famous con man by the age twenty-one. The movie "Catch Me If You Can" was his life's story of writing $2.5 million in fraudulent checks. He served five years in prison for his crimes. He was reformed by working for consulting firms and law enforcement agencies on fraud and security.

Do you feel financially hopeless due to your family's lack of legacy money or even your own at present? Reflect on the rags-to-riches stories of Andrew Carnegie, born into a family of impoverished laborers with little education. He worked his way up from a textile mill worker at age thirteen to a messenger boy and a superintendent. Carnegie invested his wealth and became the richest man in the world after he sold his Carnegie Steel Company to J. P. Morgan for $480 million.

These are two examples of how our money culture from a young age can directly impact how we respond to money in our adult life and the capacity for change. Our family had very humble beginnings. I remember playing outside in a yard full of sand on Indian Street. I walked on wooden floors with a tin roof and never knew there was better. We took pride in raking the dirt and seeing track lines with no greenery except the neighborhood's big trees. Then we moved up when mom and dad bought a house in a new neighborhood that was being developed for low-income families with dirt roads, which were eventually paved. We felt rich. What was that feeling about? We were relating money to assets and lifestyle. Was this a prelude to my financial future and view of money? Many parents, including my own, in the neighborhood, wanted more and better for us. I would say that understanding what money was and was not from our parents, teachers, and community leaders would play a big role in our future outcomes.

CHAPTER TWO

VIEW OF MONEY AS A CHILD

My views and relationship with money stem directly from my parents and upbringing. Mom and dad never talked about money in front of us kids. We never saw them exchange money between them. In those days, at least in my community, kids were seen and not heard. We were not invited into adult conversations. We had a decent two-income family, and dad ensured mom drove a nice car and would trade her car in every three years. Our parents were big on education, and a "C" on our report card was unacceptable. We lived in survival mode with hot food on the table daily and our biggest feast on Sunday. All of that was good, but what about money lessons?

As I recall, my first experience with saving money was the cute little plastic piggy bank that, for some reason, never got full. Did you have a piggy bank as a child? Today kids are taught to keep spending jars. After watching a few episodes of *Leave It to Beaver*, we asked our parents for an allowance. We had never heard of this allowance until we saw Beaver get his allowance on TV. We were overjoyed that our parents gave us an allowance of twenty-five cents a week after hearing our petitions. We were so excited to drop those coins in our piggy bank. The first thing we wanted to do was spend the money. We couldn't wait to shake money out of "piggy" and walk down to the corner neighborhood store to buy candy. At that point, I had learned how to count my change and would not be short-changed again. I am not sure why our parents did not stress saving at that point. The whole allowance was new to them as they had not had that privilege growing up. On one episode of *Leave It to Beaver*, Beaver got a raise. What do you think we did when we saw that? We asked mom and dad for a raise. They were learning a few things about how we spent our money by then. They agreed to go up to fifty cents a week, but we had to work for it. Work! Yes, we had to wipe down walls, mop our terrazzo floors, dust the house and wash dishes. We hated it. What happened to the fun of getting money and blowing it? The party was over. It was nice earning double the money and having more to spend. Once a year, dad gave us $50 each to buy anything we wanted. That would be the equivalent of approximately $500 today. I wish I had been a nerdy penny pincher, but I was not. I spent every penny of it. I remember buying a Suzy Homemaker Kitchen and a Juliet 45" record player. I also think that mom and dad felt like they were allowing us to have the things they did not have as kids. Our parents could only teach us what they had been taught. Parents, this is a great time to think about the money lessons and the value of assets that you are passing on to your children.

We learned a hard lesson about the word *loan*. One of the teachers at mom's school was doing a charity drive for children and asked mom if we had any toys we could loan out to less fortunate kids to play with during the summer. Mom always taught us good moral lessons and asked if we wanted to help these kids voluntarily. We all said yes and pulled out our very best toy to donate with the understanding that we would get these toys back. I had just purchased my beautiful China doll with long black silky straight hair. She was about 20" tall. I handed her over with pride. A few months passed, and we began to question mom about the return of our toys. Mom had gone to this teacher several times regarding returning our toys. Finally, the teacher arranged for mom to stop by her house to pick up our toys. Mom allowed us to go with her in the car. When mom returned to the car, she had an unfortunate look. She apologized to us as she handed each of us our toys. Someone had cut my doll's hair to her ears and stripped her naked of her clothes and shoes, and drew with crayons all over her body. I was visibly upset and couldn't understand why this had happened. Mom said she would never allow anything like that to happen again. I would say that I dislike the word *loan* for a long time, and I could see how people could abuse that arrangement. Adults may have similar experiences when we loan tools and books. Sometimes they never come back the way they went out. Cold hard cash can be the same way. Sometimes you never get it back, or maybe you get back less like my doll's hair.

Money signified ownership to us, as we got older. As teenagers, we graduated to buying bigger ticket items. My sister purchased a black and white portable TV with her annual $50, and I bought an organ. We took this ownership as power. I had no authority over my sister's TV. Sometimes I wanted to watch certain programs, and my sister said "NO." I would complain to mom, and she would say that my sister was the owner and I had to comply with her rules. I did not like her rules. I adapted to this control of assets and would only allow her to play my organ on my terms. My brother was not so much an issue because he had boy toys, and we did not bother him too much. Looking back, I wish mom and dad had taught us lessons on money and assets and financial etiquette.

> Cold hard cash can be the same way. Sometimes you never get it back.

Money took on a different meaning in high school. This is where I could see the haves and the have-nots in terms of money. I realized money could buy big things when I saw brand-new cars and shiny pick-up trucks driven by students while I rode the bus to school. That's when kids that did not have family money started to see what money looked like. I recall some of my classmates always having cash. Where was that coming from, I wondered. I had enough money to buy my lunch, and I was grateful. I made friends with this girl in my class whose father was a doctor. She invited me to spend the night at her house. My parents very cautiously said yes. I had never been inside a well-to-do home. I had sponge cake with chocolate icing for the first time. I needed to know more about what money could do. I was so excited to share my experiences with my family. It's all about exposure and teaching kids early on about how your money can work for you. Don't misunderstand. We had a nice home for our neighborhood. I never knew what else was out there other than the occasional Sunday scenic drive. Think about what you can do now to broaden your financial horizon for yourself and your family.

Money deals were being made at school that went over my head. Some kids were loaning money to each other. We never did that at home or in our neighborhood. Kids were buying things from each other and going places together that required cash. If you are a parent, it may be a good idea to have an open discussion with your kids about the movement of money in schools. Some kids were even betting and gambling on things within the student body. A naïve person could get gobbled up if they were not careful. It's the money culture effect. Peer groups can now influence the views of money that stem from home. This is where some kids have become enticed into money manipulation. Adults can fall into similar traps and lures of money. This is why having a healthy view of money and getting financial education early can save years of heartache.

> Have an open discussion with your kids about the movement of money in schools.

Today, I give my preteen granddaughter an appropriate amount of money for her age. I am teaching her to save and how to spend money wisely. I have asked her if other kids in her elementary school carry cash and if they have tried to take money from her or ask to borrow money. She shared with me her vision of being an entrepreneur, and we discussed the need for a financial business plan. She shared with me that they planned to open their own business one day. We have discussed what she will need to start that business and her long-term and short-term business goals. She and her sister have talked about where and how they will live. I have given her insight into the money she will need to accomplish these lifestyle goals. Money does not grow on trees, and kids need to know that. I have paid my granddaughter for making videos for me and doing extra work for her mom. Having financial discussions as early as possible will make a huge impact on the outcome of our children's lives. If parents do everything for them, they will never learn or appreciate how money works.

As a financial coach, I still discuss money with my adult kids. I have mailed financial books to them and shared my own experiences. Thankfully, they are doing well, and I have helped them to avoid certain financial pitfalls. They understand that they must work for their money and set their money up to work for them. I will share later in this book a few peaks and valleys that we went through and that I went through where money controlled us. We learned some money-related hard lessons.

CHAPTER THREE

SAVING MONEY GROWING UP

Returning to my childhood, we learned to save money once we earned an income. All three of us had jobs by the time we were fifteen years old. Mom took us to the bank to open up individual savings accounts for each of us. She told us to save our money and withhold only about $5 or $10 per paycheck for pocket money. We listened, and by the time we were each eighteen years of age, we had enough money to pay cash for our car. I remember paying $2,500 for my car. That would be about $13,000 today. Not bad for a teenager. We were not educated on establishing credit or getting a bank or car loan. We did not have much in the way of expenses as we lived at home for a while. This would have been a great time to start a financial game plan and have our money working for us. I carried on this generational view of money with my kids.

By the time my kids were old enough to purchase a vehicle, their peers were buying cars on credit. Like his buddies, my son pressured me to help him get a car loan. His friends had even coached him on where to buy car insurance. One of his friends came home to a barely used automobile sitting in the driveway. A cream puff, they called it. This friend had not worked, had not saved, and had no financial skin in the game to get this car. At that time, in my kids' eyes, I looked like such a bad parent for asking them to work to earn things in life. I was teaching them the money culture that was handed down to me by my parents. Have you ever had to stand your financial ground with family or friends?

Persistence paid off as our children took on employment as teenagers and paid cash for their first automobiles. I recall my son eating ramen noodles for six months and banking 99% of his paycheck because he wanted to purchase a car priced beyond the $2,500 cap I set. I would not supplement the car budget. I told him he would have to work harder to pay for what he wanted. He would need more of his hard-earned money if he wanted a more expensive car. He was not willing to settle for less. He saved an additional $1,500 for a total of $4,000 and was ready to purchase a hot little sports car. He found the perfect car online, not far away. The private owner asked $4700, which was way out of my son's range. I agreed to go and look at the car, but I knew this was out of his league. Of course, in the back of his mind, he thought I would supplement the difference. This car was clean and in mint condition. The owner was a young lady in the military who had kept the car in her garage while she was away on duty. My son wanted that car badly, but I told him right before the owner that this car was beyond his means. I told her that he only had $4000 cash saved up. At that moment, my son gave me this strong disgruntled look and whispered to me with his teeth gritted that I was ruining his purchase, asking me why I didn't loan him the money? The car owner was watching us, and I turned to her and repeated that we couldn't purchase the car because my son did not have enough money. She stared at me and stated, "I will sell you the car for $4,000." My son was ecstatic! This car was worth more than she was asking for, even at $4700. We both thanked this young woman for working with us. I was happy that I taught him to stay within budget. I felt like he had learned a lesson that day. Buy what you can afford and there are good-hearted people in this world.

I am on board with paying cash for a car, as this is a depreciating asset. I like the idea of saving money and buying what you can afford. There are times when a car loan may be the only option. In this case, shop wisely and understand the difference in principal, interest and methods of interest rate calculations such as fixed. Also understand the the Rule of 78 in which the borrower pays a big chunk of the interest in the early cycle of the loan. Simple interest maybe a better option as the interest is calculated off of the principal balance with a set monthly principle and interest monthly payment. Neither one of our kids had car loans when they lived at home. My son lived with me at home while attending college. He came home one day and said he wanted to buy a motorcycle in addition to already owning a car. Once again, his buddies were encouraging him to finance the purchase. My answer was the same, save your money. At this point, he did not like me very much. He thought I was trying to make it hard for him to purchase the bike. Of course, I did not want him to get the bike, but that was not the issue. My son took it on the chin, scheduled more shifts at work and saved $3,700 cash to purchase the motorcycle. He is happy and I stood my ground on saving money and living within his means. These were just the beginnings of discussions on saving money with our kids. You can see how we teach our kids smart money lessons and the value of listening to people with experience. We know the money pitfalls that they have yet to experience. Of course, at some point in their lives, they will get financially bit, as we all do, but that is a part of life and gaining wisdom.

Credit is not a bad option. I was not taught how to use credit to one's advantage. Sometimes, a car loan at 2% interest may be better than taking money out of an investment account, earning 4-8% interest. I don't recall any of my teachers in school preparing us on how money works and how to manage credit. I can't speak for all colleges; however, I can say that when I attended college, I did not take any courses on how to balance cash and credit for daily living. There are finance classes that teach you about how interest rates are determined and various lending methods and payoff strategies. As a young married couple, we had racked up a lot of credit card debt due to a lack of understanding of long-term financial loss. I had learned how to save my money and buy a car with cash, but credit cards were being given out like water, and it was easy to swipe the card and pay later. My parents couldn't teach me much about credit cards because of the generation gap in this new craze.

In my grandparent's generation and many present-day cultures, money is hidden all over the house. I don't want to give away secret storage spaces for security reasons, but I know of families that could access tens of thousands of dollars on their property. Think of this for a moment. If your money is kept safely with you at home, how can it grow? Some people refer to this as having access to quick cash. Haven't you seen movies where even wealthy people have elaborate safes in their homes? Where is the logic of growing money with this practice? Perhaps they have acquired enough cash to have a surplus at their fingertips. Some cultures generationally teach you to keep your money where you can put your hands on it. Money can't grow and multiply in these cases, and a family passes on stagnating assets. We were taught to put our money in a checking account for expenses and a saving account for storing our money (not growing it). Some people don't trust banks, or each other for that matter. Some people don't like carrying cash on them for fear of robbery. There have been times when I had to carry a large amount of cash on me because I had just sold a big item. I would be in a cold sweat until I could get to the bank to deposit the cash. I felt completely naked and transparent, as if everyone knew I was carrying cold hard cash with me. Can you relate to this feeling? This fear of money is related to my money culture. Why don't I feel elated when I have a stack of cash in my hands?

Saving money is a great component of a financial game plan. We must be strategic about the elements of saving. Establish a purpose for the savings. Are you saving for a car, house, vacation, college, or a planned medical procedure? Let us not forget the emergency fund account, which must be accessible immediately. There are instances where an emergency travel situation might occur that will require you to travel due to a life-and-death situation. I recall when a distant family member suddenly passed away, and one of their offspring couldn't afford to travel to the funeral to pay their last respects to their parent. This was heartbreaking for everyone. Be realistic about your financial needs. When will you need to touch the money? Time frames will determine if you can avoid certain fees on longer-term savings and growing products. Your age also determines this. Suppose you are in your teens and twenties. In that case, you are undoubtedly acquiring certain assets where you will want quick and easy access to your cash, like a small savings account or a healthy money market or CD (certificates of deposit) product for larger value items. If you are somewhat settled and have a home with an ample income stream, you may decide its best to place your money in a growth investing/retirement type product. These individualized financial choices should be discussed with a financially licensed professional. We will go into more detail on these options later in this book.

CHAPTER FOUR

FREEDOM TO DISCUSS MONEY

Our early experiences of money are how we will carry the torch into our own families. My parents did not prepare us for the big financial picture. They did not talk about budgeting or investing. We might have had different financial outcomes if we had started investing early. I did not learn about that until my first child graduated from high school. Think about all the opportunities that passed me by financially to grow my money and have a secure financial future. Several years ago, I began to read financial books, and much of the don'ts in those books applied to me. I have made a 360-degree turn in my life financially and have lived experiences to share that can be a resource to educate others. What I share with you in this book, including my personal money stories, are for educational purposes only and not to be construed as financial advice.

My parents taught us to be hush-hush about our financial earnings. "Never tell anyone how much you make. Don't discuss your money with anyone," I was told. This almost created a fear of money, like it was taboo or someone would take it away from me. This fear of discussing money is why I had a mental block as an adult against speaking with a financial coach. In my adult life, some friends shared their incomes, investments, entrepreneurial interest, and financial successes and failures. As I mentioned earlier, in my home and my neighborhood, those discussions did not happen. In hindsight, I can see how this was a hindrance. We did not have any building blocks. We couldn't grow mentally in money management and financial planning. My acquired insight is what we plant and water is what will grow. What are you planting and watering right now for yourself and your family financially?

My dad worked two jobs, and my mom worked in the school system. We never knew why dad was gone so much. He worked at the phone company during the day and had several cleaning jobs at night and on the weekends. We would see him for an hour when he would come home to eat dinner, and then he was gone again. We were a family of five living in an average minority neighborhood, just trying to survive. We did not know that mom and dad were spread thin financially. All we knew was that we were happy and had clothes and food. I don't recall hearing money discussions between my parents, they kept that behind closed doors. They never explained prices to us when we went shopping and how to bargain shop, although I think that is because we shopped at discount stores. I was the oldest child and the first among my siblings to attend high school. Before starting my first year in high school, I recall when my mother took me downtown to a store called Flossie's. This was where upscale people shopped. She wanted me to have some nice clothes to wear. I learned later that mom had to save a lot of money for me to have that shopping experience. I wish I had been taught the value of money at the time. Maybe I would have appreciated her sacrifice. Parents, I am sure many of you have told your children the financial cost of something when they appear not to appreciate what you have done for them or given them. At that moment, they can't even relate to what you are saying. Of course, you sense that in your frustration. The best course of action is to teach our children along the way early about money, assets and values. And don't forget – try having them work for it.

> What we plant and water is what will grow.

The big spend occurred when I was graduating from high school. That is when I found out that we did not have a lot of money. Class rings, caps, gowns, grad night at Walt Disney World and the senior cruise - my parents couldn't afford those things. Of course, not understanding money and its value made this hard for me to digest. I had to work hard to save money for my class ring and senior pictures. By high school, the student body was integrated and kids from affluent neighborhoods were able to order top-of-line rings while others students couldn't purchase anything. That is when I began to see a class distinction determined by money. The time came for the senior cruise, which I begged my parents to let me go on, of course on their dime. My dad said no! Mom was a softy and she promised me a cruise. I did not go on the senior cruise with my classmates. Mom recently confided in me that she saved her money for a year and bumped heads with dad on the matter. She said they would get into big arguments about the expenditure, but she was determined that my siblings and me would have that cruise experience, so we went as a family. The cool part about it was we cruised on a nicer ship than the student body called *The Emerald Seas*, which sailed from 1992 and retired in 2009. We sailed out a week or two after the class senior cruise excursion which gave me great bragging rights.

Money shouldn't be a secret from our kids. I teach my granddaughter all the time about money. She is eleven years old which is a great time to learn how to manage money. Recently, I gave her $10 for good grades in school. She wanted to go to the $5 and below store to spend her gift. I explained to her that there would be a tax on $10. I put a $20 bill in her hand as I did not have any $1 bills. I told her to only spend $10 plus tax, and to bring my change home. Great money lesson, right? Things did not go as planned. She spent the $20, under my husband's urging, and in fact her total bill was $29 and he paid for the overage. I had to teach her a hard lesson. I reminded her of our arrangement and that she owed me some change. I asked her to pull out all of the items that she had purchased along with her receipt. I instructed her

> Money shouldn't be a secret from our kids.

to pick out the items that she wanted to keep and the items that we would return to the store. My husband thought that I was being mean and urged me just to let it go. I knew that my granddaughter would never forget this experience and it was teaching her a principal that would last her a lifetime. Children need to understand that there are boundaries with money. Adults, we need to respect our own financial limitations as well. Stay inside of your financial game plan.

Back in the day, in our community, most homes had the Big White Bible. This was where my parents kept all their important documents. Mom had her will and her insurance papers. This guy called "the insurance man" came to our house every week to get money from my mom. I don't know how much or what the meaning of it was. All we knew was that he wore a white dress shirt and some nice pants. Who was this insurance man? Mom never told us much about him at that time. When my dad passed away, my mother said she couldn't bear to spend his death benefit. She put the money into a fund that one of her co-workers told her about. I found out about this twenty-five years later. Right after my dad passed away, when I was married with my small kids, my mom cashed the individual insurance policies she had taken out on the three of us.

We never knew anything about those policies. She gave each one of us $1,500 for our policies. I did not quite understand what was happening. Mom did not teach us about insurance, so I never purchased insurance for my kids other than what was offered at work. Looking back, $1,500 over about twenty years was not the best money multiplier. My parents did their best based on the information they had at the time. At least she had something to pass on to us. My mother has a similar policy for herself that she has been paying on for over fifty years! This policy has a very low death benefit; however, at her age, it's probably best to keep it. All I can say is a good job, mom because you did something rather than doing nothing. As a financial coach, I see how the lack of education can hurt families and generations. Mom and dad should have told us more about the insurance man. I am sure I would have secured life insurance for my kids and husband and taught them to do the same during those family years.

How often in today's times do husbands and wives discuss money privately and pass on money lessons to their children? There are times when adults and parents should have private money conversations. Financial literacy is still a growing concern in our society. Sometimes the real deal on money is not discovered until a family break up, like a divorce or separation. The court system typically requires the husband and wife to disclose all financial accounts and assets in detail on a financial statement.

Sometimes, one mate has hidden money in secret accounts, or one mate will withdraw funds from a joint account without notice. We will discuss those liberties later on in this book. The same can happen in partnerships when money is concealed through fancy footwork and financial statements. Some couples have weekly financial discussions and cover all income and expenses. This is a great example of not being in fear of discussing money. You have heard it said that knowledge is power. The more you know about your family finances, the better control you will have over them.

CHAPTER FIVE

LIFESTYLE

When you hear the word lifestyle, what comes to your mind? For me, these words ring with financial security and contentment. It means financial freedom with the ability to choose your time and where and how you live. Countries and regions are known for certain lifestyles that attract tourism from all over the world. What about the sandy beaches of Hawaii with bursting colors of the rainbow in floral print surrounded by beautiful waters? Many people work their entire lives to gain the option to spend their retirement years sipping their favorite libation while enchanting island music plays. When I was divorced after twenty years of marriage, I gifted myself a trip to Hawaii. This was my dream trip to see how other people live. I believe that we need our senses opened to experience various cultures, foods, mountainous regions, oceans, people and money exchanges.

According to Investopedia, "The U.S. Dollar is considered the most powerful or strongest currency in the world."[1] And according to Financebuzz.com, "As of March 2022, the US was the strongest in Peru, with approximately 3.72 Peruvian soles needed to make one dollar."[2] Recently, when a family member visited the Bahamas, they were given $600 in Bahamian money. A smart financial move would have been to exchange the currency for the U.S. Dollar before leaving the island. Upon returning to the States, the cost of the exchange resulted in a net amount of $400 in U.S. cash. This is just a small lesson in understanding lifestyle, money, and international spending. Get to know your cash exchanges before you travel abroad.

The television series *Lifestyle of the Rich and Famous* caught the world's attention as millionaires and billionaires allowed us to view their posh, sprawling estates. This certainly created a want of heart. How realistic is it that any of us can live without a care in the world financially? How much money does owning a 14 Karat gold bathroom take? What about an infinity pool in your living room? I would say that this type of living did not come without some financial planning and wealth management. Actor Jim Carrey wrote himself a check for $10 million before he had $10 dollars in his pocket. This was his visual incentive to one day cash that check, and ten years later, his dream came true when he was cast in the movie "Dumb and Dumber." Maintaining a desired lifestyle takes a financial game plan, goals, patience, and time. Even for families where money is inherited, making smart financial choices is critical to sustaining that lucrative lifestyle. Securing a solid financial team is a good start, including an accountant, financial coach/advisor, estate planner, and tax professional. This team makes for great planning, growth, and money protection.

In my world, all I had on my team was my tax accountant. I was never exposed to other professionals. I did not know what a financial advisor did. When I worked in corporate America, several of my peers in upper management spoke of working with a financial professional. They were smarter than me because they were planning their future financial lives. They knew they would need to build up their cash and have it grow for them long-term so they could have the life they wanted when retirement rolled around. Several key employees offered to refer me to their financial professional, but I declined. I was afraid of money and certainly afraid to talk about money because of my upbringing. I thought these financial professionals wanted something from me to get into my business. I ran from them because I thought I did not need them. Perhaps I may have thought that I was financially insignificant. In my mind, I was not wealthy and had little money, so why did I need to talk to a financial person? There are people like me who, through a lack of early exposure, are not open to working with a financial professional. I get it and understand them.

There is a trust factor that bonds clients to professionals and gets stronger over time. My current lifestyle is one that fell into place because I did not take the time to plan for it. Have you heard it said, "Either you make a decision, or one will be made for you"? Financial outcomes happen for all of us each day, whether we participate in the decisions or not. Take a moment and look at your current lifestyle. Is this where you want to be? If not, what are you willing to do to get there? Understand that nothing happens overnight and that you will get nothing if you do nothing.

> There is a trust factor that bonds clients to professionals and gets stronger over time.

Some wheels should be set in motion to lock down your financial outcomes. One component is estate planning, which ensures protection and control over one's estate during and after death. For full legal protection, you may want to work with an estate attorney who can prepare properly executable wills, trust funds, power of attorney documents, and guidance on avoiding probate costs. I have heard horror stories of estates being lost to unpaid tax bills or unscrupulous family members not acting in good financial faith. Have you heard it said that money could unmask people? I have even heard of unauthorized family members moving into the home of deceased parents or relatives and not paying rent or mortgage payments. The other surviving siblings or relatives have engaged law enforcement and the legal system to have the unauthorized family member removed from the property. Creditors can come out of the woodwork and attach liens to properties when

> Some wheels should be set in motion to lock down your financial outcomes.

the owner passes away. Be prepared to have forward thinking and put measures in place so that you have the final say over your estate.

Establishing life insurance offers income protection for households when a stream of income is halted due to death, disability, and critical and chronic illness. This is another method of preserving your lifestyle. In the US, most employers offer employees basic group life insurance for a low payroll deduction rate. The downside to this is that in most cases, when your employment is severed, so is the life insurance. Perhaps you worked for your former company for five to fifteen years and found the need to purchase life insurance on your own. Factors that raise the cost of life insurance are age and health history. As we age, many of us start to have a few medical conditions that may or may not require treatment, prescriptions, therapies, and surgeries. We will discuss how life insurance can offer a source of income while you still live later in this book.

Retirement planning is another method of financial planning that ensures you will have the lifestyle you desire in later years. In my former mindset, retirement meant someone in their late 60s to mid-70s. That said, I was not the least interested in discussing retirement income when I was in my 20s, 30s, and 40s—being undereducated translated into being underfunded for a stream of income when my career of forty-one years ended unexpectedly due to the pandemic. I couldn't go to Hawaii on my retirement dollars. A major lifestyle change was occurring right before my eyes. In hindsight, I did not listen when the subject of financial planning was brought up. Utilizing my insight, I have since made all the right moves by getting my license as a financial coach, setting up my retirement plans, and helping communities and households do the same. We will talk about retirement options later in this book.

Let's briefly discuss caregiving as part of our outlook on lifestyles. Have you given much thought to your aging parents and their health needs? What about your spouse's or your significant other's health as the aging process sets in? You may to consider some options that offer financial solutions to help offset the cost of care. There are disability riders that can be attached to life insurance policies and retirement plans. Wellbeing riders offer the policy owner/insured options of penalty-free withdrawals from various financial products. Long-term care policies and riders offer the policy owner/insured nursing home and/or assisted living care. These option can be a really big deal when you think of the fulltime mental, physical and financial resources that are needed to care for loved ones.

As you may now see, financial preparedness is one of the biggest keys to ensuring that we have the lifestyle we desire. Bankruptcy is a huge disrupter. According to statistics, approximately 66% of all bankruptcy is due to the cost of medical care in later years. Imagine a husband, wife, or significant other needing extensive, costly therapies, prescriptions, walkers, and wheelchairs. Social Security will not be enough as this barely covers the cost of living. If you have attained the covered age, Medicare can be of some help but does not cover 100% of everything. During these times, with the high cost of medical care, the residential home may be at financial risk, and extended families may have to assist. Much of this demise can be preventable with a solid financial plan that covers those golden years. There is no time like the present to start taking a financial inventory of what we have and what we don't want to lose and consulting with a financial professional. Remember these are long-term goals, so allow yourself plenty of time, years in most cases, to set up a secure financial future.

MONEY TO
BURN OR
BE BURNED

Money to Burn or Be Burned

Loaning Money

Signing Your Name

Giving Money Away

Shared Accounts

CHAPTER SIX

MONEY TO BURN
OR BE BURNED

When you hear the word *burn,* what comes to mind? Usually, this denotes a fire of property, a painful physical experience or the permanent destruction of something. What about referring to money and the word *burn*? Have you heard the phrase "He's got money to burn"? What does that mean to you? For me, the phrase means an overabundance of cash to the point that if you lost some, you would not lament over it. This phrase could also be interpreted as a flagrancy or showy display of one's means of life. Or does it? These views are certainly open to interpretation. We can compare another phrase: "Money is burning a hole in their pocket." This meaning could imply the inability to hold on to one's cash. There is the more detrimental phrase: "I got burned." In the financial world, "getting burned" refers to an unforeseen financial loss with ill intent on one or more parties involved. Have you experienced the "Financial Burn" in either of these scenarios? Let's explore for deeper meaning.

What is the origin of "Money to Burn?" One possible origin is the result of a consultation between two businesspeople in Rochester, NY, of which an article was written in the *Los Angeles Herald*, Volume 44,

Number 82, 2 July 1895.[3] The story goes that a prominent, well-to-do merchant in New York was engaging in a business conversation with a promoter regarding a large project that would need substantial funding. After hearing the project's magnitude, the merchant commented, "You will need a large sum of cash" to the promoter. The promoter pulled out a handful of cash, twisted it, threw it up, lit his cigar, and burned it. Stunned by this arrogance, the merchant stated, "that was a $10 bill"! The promoter acknowledged so without a care. A year later, at a dining establishment, a mutual businessman attempted to introduce the promoter to the merchant when the merchant stated he did not need an introduction. He said, referring to the promoter, "He has money to burn." Can we see the inference of "money to burn" in that story? "Money to burn" was considered pompous and less desirable in business. We want to be good stewards of our money, understanding that our community will form attachments or detachments depending on their perception and money culture. Of course, this does not disparage those with abundant money; we celebrate you with a job well done for your excellent wealth management. A financial coach/advisor is always in the background, helping channel those extra resources to charity, community enrichment, and the portfolio income bucket.

"He just got a windfall of cash, and that money is burning a hole in his pocket." We can smile when we hear this expression because sometimes you want to blow the money! Some people get paid on Friday, and the money is gone by Monday. This can be hard on families when the primary breadwinner can't hang on to the cash. Merchants can count on people spending their sizeable income tax refunds. Have you ever noticed how many financial lures are advertised between January and March? Cars, vacations, and business venture opportunities are plentiful. Notice I said *spend*. Some people don't have the mindset to save and multiply their money. I recall a young couple who received a large sum of money from the wife's deceased mother's life insurance policy, and within a year, the entire amount was gone. Think about people who hit the lottery. Most of them are broke within five years of receiving the big payout. In 2011, Gerald Muswagon out of Canada became an instant millionaire with a lottery ticket. Within a few years, he was broke due to lavish spending and some legal trouble. A more positive outcome could be achieved if we consider not spending but rather ways to grow this money into more money. Of course, we want to reward ourselves within reason and in line with our financial game plan.

The saddest of the "burn" is involuntarily having our money burned. This unwelcome outcome can lead people into financial ruin. Have you ever heard of a Ponzi scheme? Bernie Madoff is historically one of the most high-profile convicted Ponzi schemers. It is estimated that unsuspecting victims lost approximately 50 billion in about twenty years. I recall watching stories such as *American Greed*, interviewing people who had been tricked and lost their life savings, homes, retirement money, and children's college funds. They were left broke with no financial restitution in sight. I have lost money in things that appeared to render me a boatload of money, only to lose that money in the end.

I did not do research on the players, the presenters, the company, and the product. I swallowed the pill and got burned. I received a call from a friend who said they had a line on an excellent way to double my money in six months. Telling me a mutual friend told them about it. My close friend said our mutual friend vouched for the head honcho and that he had business-savvy credentials. I did Google the head honcho but couldn't validate much other than he existed. Call me naive or just plain dumb, but I wired $3,000 to this bank account per the instructions of someone I did not personally know. My friends were duped also. They were very embarrassed when within four months, this business venture folded. The head honcho promised he would repay everyone. That was eight years ago, and I have not seen a penny of my money. I take full responsibility for what happened to me, as I should have been more responsible. As a financial coach, I educate people on working with licensed professionals regarding their hard-earned money. We say in our industry, never take financial guidance from someone not legally credentialed.

> Never take financial guidance from someone not legally credentialed.

What does money look like? Do we stereotype people financially? Some people use cash to make friends and to feel important. Throwing lavish parties, always picking up food and beverage tabs, jet-setting and being in the limelight feels good to them. Others try to keep up with the lucrative lifestyles but are not financially positioned to do so and live in the negative financially, paycheck to paycheck. The look of money can significantly impact how we handle our cash. Have you ever seen that guy or that girl who tells you how much money they have when you meet them? It's the "I have" syndrome. I have a house on the hill and a luxury sports car; I have an elite membership; this is my designer shirt, designer handbag, and the list goes on. The wise and savvy person lays low, and you will learn more about them as your relationship grows. I share a story I read about a man who walked into a high-end car dealership dressed as if he'd just come off the beach. No one made time to speak with him. He finally caused a stir in management and told them he was a millionaire and would never purchase a car from them. The staff had stereotyped this man and lost a customer. This begs the question: Why do we as a society have to wear our money? What about where we live?

A millionaire friend said they dreamed of having it all and finally did. They purchased their million-dollar home with more rooms than they ever had under one roof. They had a staff, a nanny, chefs, maids and everything but happiness. They realized that the look of money was not what they desired after all. No one came to their home unless they threw lavish dinner parties. They sold that house and decided to rent, and have their money working for them, gaining more family flexibility and quality time together. Their experience had a significant impact on me. Understand where you are going financially and why. We are by no means saying it's bad to live lavishly and have all the spoils of life. We are saying, find what makes you happy, not what other people expect you to have. I have another friend who recently told me that she is constantly finding ways to increase her multiple streams of income. She is financially free and prosperous and chooses to live modestly, travel, and eat fabulously. I love her motto. You can't see her money, you can only see how she enjoys it.

> Understand where you are going financially and why.

We have discussed how money can fall through our fingers at will or by deceit. The intentions of this book are for you to take a personal inventory of yourself and how you view money. What is your relationship with money? How do you want people to perceive you when it comes to money? When speaking to audiences, I share that I have more money now than when I was working in corporate America. They look at me in shock, and then I say, let me rephrase that statement. Through financial education and lived experiences of *Hindsight to Insight*, I am retaining more of my money now than when I had more and was spending more. You have heard it said that it's not how much money you have, it's how much money you keep. My goal is to open your eyes to keeping your money and allowing it to work for you. It's okay to be picky about pulling out the green and paying for things you may get a better bargain price elsewhere. At some high-end restaurants, you get less food and spend more money. Of course, we want to be mindful of the quality of our food. We are learning the value of financial empowerment and ways to keep more of our money.

CHAPTER SEVEN

LOANING MONEY

My first official loan was a car I financed in my twenties. I had never filled out paperwork before to borrow money. This process was very intimidating and nerve-racking. I did not understand this lengthy contract with places for my initials and signature. There were "spaces" for the loan amount and other numbers that increased the loan, which seemed to me to be a formality. If you have ever applied for a loan, you know that feeling of waiting on pins and needles for the words "your loan is approved!" Then the fun begins when the first payment (installment) is due. What comes to mind when you hear the words *loan money*?

Some people may think of a banking institution or a lending company. Hundreds of companies offer loans without seeing the borrower virtually or in person. What is a loan? In simple terms, a financial loan is a debt, money owed over a set period. Merriam-Webster's dictionary defines a loan as "Money lent at interest" and "something usually lent for the borrower's temporary use."[4] In the formal lending world, a loan has many components for the borrower and the lender. The lender sets the terms and the qualifications of the loan. The original amount of money being borrowed is referred to as the principal. This is important to understand because the amount of money due over time could exceed the principal amount. Some factors could increase the borrower's obligation to pay the amount. The lender typically is in the business of loaning money and offsets the cost of doing business by assessing fees such as loan origination fees, application fees, late fees, processing fees, finance charges and interest charges throughout the loan.

Loan applications are required in most cases to establish creditworthiness, which is an assessment of the borrower's ability to repay the loan. Some loans may require collateral (secured loan) based on the borrower's credit history and credit score. Collateral is a financial asset that offers the lender security and protects the lender if the borrower defaults, which could result in the asset being repossessed. An unsecured loan means the borrower has a good debt-to-income ratio and meets the borrowing requirements of the lender. An unsecured loan is also referred to as a signature loan. After the application is processed, the loan is either offered to the borrower or declined. If a loan is provided, the mode of payment is outlined, weekly, monthly, quarterly, yearly or whatever is agreed upon. Of utmost importance is that this agreement takes the form of signed documents (contract) between the lender and borrower that legally protects both borrower and lender. The terms and conditions processes are put in place to reduce risk to the lender. What about loaning money without contracts, a credit review, application or collateral, sometimes called verbal agreements?

> Loaning money between families can be complicated and, in some cases, dicey.

Loaning money between families can be complicated and, in some cases, dicey. My husband and I were trying to buy a home and needed money in the bank. We had not planned to buy a house and had not saved any significant money for this investment. A bomb was dropped on us when our apartment lease was terminated early when the owner was sent home from the military earlier than planned. He wanted to live in his duplex, and we couldn't blame him for that. We only had four or five months to find a new place to live. We decided to try buying rather than renting because we did not like our lack of control as renters. This was well over thirty years ago, and there are laws regarding borrowed money in the purchasing process. My mother agreed to loan us $500 to have in the bank, and to my surprise, she asked us to sign a promissory note to repay the money without interest, in full by a specific date. This request for a contract felt awkward to me. After all, this was my mother. Didn't she trust me? Of course, the reality hit me, we had to pay the money back as agreed. We did get our first home, and we did repay the loan to my mother according to the terms of the loan. My mother taught me a lesson on setting terms and getting signed agreements that I will share with you later in this book.

Sometimes, a family member may deny your request for a loan. My household income shrank when I divorced and became a single parent of two kids. My son had come into some money from a car accident, and I thought he would be too happy to lend me some money to get by. He was still living at home by this time in his early twenties while attending a local college. I felt a little weird asking my child for money. Shouldn't I be caring for him, being a financially strong parent? We sat in the living room, and I said I needed to ask him for a favor. He sat quietly as I continued to ask him for several thousand dollars as a loan. His reaction surprised me. He said, "Mom, that's a lot of money." In my world, that amount was peanuts compared to my monthly income and expenditures, but to him, it was like asking for $100,000. This request made him uneasy. I explained to him that this was temporary and that I would repay the loan promptly. He said this did not feel right, and I told him to forget I had asked. I am sure he did not want to hurt me, but this was too much to ask of him. Word to the wise, never do anything you don't understand or feel good about financially. Looking back, I am happy that he did not become a lender to his mother. This taught me not to presume family will be willing to loan to you. Just because you may know how much money a family member has does not give you financial entitlement.

Loaning between friends has its dynamics that can have long-term relationship effects. Friends are somewhat different from family members who, due to bloodlines, may be more forgiving when loans go delinquent, not paid in full or at all. I remembered my mother's lesson about signing paperwork when loaning money, so my first loan to a friend followed that process. My girlfriend needed $2500 to catch up on rent, and her income was short due to her employer not getting money from a client on time. She was slightly uncomfortable when I asked her to sign papers, but she complied. After the transaction, I felt uneasy because now I was a lender and had no guarantee of getting this money back in my hands. I must admit I worried about this loan as I agreed to a lump sum repayment without interest. In hindsight, I did not assess my friend's ability to repay; this was purely an emotional "I got you" loan. This was a risky move on my part. The good news is that she did repay the loan, and I felt so much better after that. Of course, this experience gave me a false sense of the lending risk exposure that I would later learn about.

The personal loan landscape had a different outcome that has stuck with me. I was starting a new business in which I invested about $2700 to purchase products. I was excited about this venture and felt pretty good about the income potential. I shared the opportunity with a male friend, and he, too, saw the business potential and wanted to get started. The only caveat was that he did not have the financial start-up cash. Feeling quite confident in the business, my level of commitment to recover my ROI (Return On Investment), and my belief that my male friend shared the same level of commitment, I offered to loan him the money to get started. Why not help a friend, right? I did the usual by getting him to sign a promissory note, but I did not have any terms or time frames, only that it was a non-interest-bearing loan that would become due once he started working the business and bringing in income. The problem is that he never started working the business, meaning he never earned any business income to repay me, and he had about $2700 worth of product that never got into customers' hands. I was in utter disbelief that this was happening. What about our friendship, the whole trust factor? He never made any financial payment or restitution to me. Here is the uncomfortable part, do I take him to court and ruin our long-term friendship ties? Or maybe I was hoping that one day his conscience would kick in, and he would acknowledge the financial loan default, and he would make an attempt to repay me. I opted to avoid court, and I was too embarrassed to share this experience with anyone and never spoke about it for years. I learned the paper is only as good as the two people who sign it and I must be willing to enforce the contract in a default situation. My friendship did change. Although we are still friends, it is a distant and untrustworthy relationship. It shouldn't surprise you that the subject of the loan never comes up. This lesson taught me that I am not a lender, and as I have heard it said, "Never loan any money that you can't afford to lose."

> Never loan any money that you can't afford to lose.

CHAPTER EIGHT

SIGNING YOUR NAME

There are ways that we can financially obligate ourselves by simply signing our names on someone else's behalf. This can be called cosigning or putting a loan in our name for someone else who is not creditworthy. Sometimes parents will cosign for a car loan or an apartment for their kids. We are talking about this situation because it can translate into cold hard cash coming out of your pocket if the person you are helping defaults. What are the financial obligations of a cosigner? Investopedia says, "A co-signer takes on the legal obligation to be a backup repayment source, reduces the risk to the lender, and helps the borrower obtain a loan."[5] Co-signing is different from co-borrowing. One of the big differences is who gets the money or principal in their hands. In the case of co-borrowing, both parties receive the principal and are responsible for the monthly payment. A co-signer is not initially responsible for the monthly payment (but is responsible for default) and does not receive the principal amount. There is considerable trust and significant risk exposure in the co-signing situation, considering the co-signer does not get the cash in a money loan or have possession of the asset. We must be careful not to make emotional money decisions when asked to co-sign and co-borrow. Remember that the promissory note is a legal document that states the co-signer and co-borrow are obligated to repay the loan in the case of default, which could happen in the event of loss of income, death, hardship or just a refusal to pay by the other party.

Co-signing for an asset like a car or an apartment can be tricky. Remember, the co-signer does not get possession. Can you imagine co-signing for a car for someone who gets into an accident, totals the car, and does not have insurance? No car, but the car loan is still legally due. Or, in my case, over twenty years ago, I co-signed a lease for a friend. She asked for help, and I had never done anything like that nor understood the risk I was putting myself in. I began to get this knot in my stomach when I had to fill out paperwork that included my income and liabilities. "What was I thinking?" I said to myself. It was too late to back out, although I wanted to revert. In the back of my mind, I was hoping I would get declined, but I had good credit, and the paperwork was approved for a one-year lease. My friend was happy. The scary part was that this person's work history was not solid, although she was a diligent worker. I had an entire year to sweat this out, hoping that this person could stay employed and not default. I decided not to co-sign for the lease renewal, even if asked. Thankfully, we survived the lease period, and I was free and clear financially. My *hindsight to insight* taught me to never co-sign for a lease ever again. This book is about understanding our money mindset with family and friends and how it can significantly impact our financial well-being.

There are medical situations that require the signature of someone to be financially responsible when the patient is incapacitated. I had never given this a second thought when signing for my kids or my husband when they needed medical care. I recommend checking the laws in your state to determine who is responsible for medical care when a non-patient signs paperwork indicating their financial responsibility. I will share an experience of such a case where a husband signed his wife into the hospital in an emergency. His wife did not survive, and the husband received bills totaling six figures from the hospital. He couldn't pay these bills and reached out for legal help. Eventually, he did come to a financial resolution. Most of us are not thinking about money when trying to help save a person's life. Sadly, money can directly impact humanitarian efforts.

Adding someone to your credit card as a co-signer is another way to open ourselves up to financial risk. Parents may add their kids to their credit cards to help the child build credit. This is not a terrible thing. However, this scenario can quickly go bad if the parent does not control the charges on the card and is not mindful of the growing balance. When we do things like this, we should always consider the pros and cons and be willing to accept a negative outcome.

When my daughter was seventeen, I added her to my credit card for several reasons. My daughter was responsible for her age, she went to school and worked part-time while living at home. To help her out, I would fill up her car with gas. Adding her name as a signer on my credit card allowed her to build credit and fuel her vehicle. I proudly put

> The time to put credit cards in a newbie's hands is when they establish creditworthiness.

this credit card in her hands. That is like putting a loaded gun in the hands of someone who has never fired a weapon. The next thing I knew, my daughter was hooked on spending sprees at the mall with her plastic in hand. The promise to pay later seemed magical to her, and I believed she could do so because she had a job. Before I knew it, she was $4,000 in debt on my credit card with no real plan to repay. She was not saving money as we had planned. I must take full responsibility for not being a better guardian of my credit card and not teaching my daughter the responsibility of buying now and paying later. In hindsight, I shouldn't have given her an actual credit card. I like the concept of helping her build credit but not create debt. Her credit would begin to grow as I paid my balance due in full or in monthly payments according to the credit card company's terms. The time to put credit cards in a newbie's hands is when they establish creditworthiness.

In the end, I ended up taking the card away from her and paying the debt. I handled my son differently when he came of age. Once, he had a job, and while still living at home, on the advice of my accountant, I took him to a jewelry store and instructed him to make a small purchase and apply for store financing. He purchased me a beautiful pair of sterling silver heart-shaped earrings for $100. A gift for me! I thought he would indeed buy something for his girlfriend. He diligently made his payments on time. Credit is money, and we are learning unique ways to manage our cash and positively teach our kids the same.

Sometimes we allow ourselves to take on financial exposure when we don't fast forward and think about the consequences if the absolute worst happens. We were planning a family reunion many years ago, and I volunteered to be the coordinator. I had experience organizing corporate events, so this was a piece of cake. We planned a week's worth of activities. I secured a hotel and set up a nice poolside reception room for the day of arrival, with refreshments and appetizers. I signed a contract with the hotel, including my credit card, to secure a block of ten rooms for the week. There was no money down then, but a percentage of money would be due as the check-in date drew closer. Everyone was excited, as many traveled from out of state to attend. We planned this event about six months in advance. The thread started unraveling about two or three months before check-in. Family members began canceling for medical reasons. I was in shock! I re-read the contract and discovered I was financially responsible for at least 50 % of the room block, translating into about $5,000 out of my pocket! This was a nightmare. I called the hotel, explained the situation, and asked to be removed from the contract. Keep in mind that the hotel had held these rooms for months, and they were financially impacted by not releasing them. The hotel board met and offered me out of the contract with a $1,000 invoice to me! This bill was solely on me because I signed the contract. I went to the family members and informed them of the financial consequences of the cancellation. Ultimately, we banded together, sharing the bill by $100 each. Be careful in what you sign and know the monetary terms of cancellation and default. Financial heartache is tough, and I hope my experience can save you money.

CHAPTER NINE

GIVING MONEY AWAY

Money is transferable, meaning it passes from one person or entity to another with or without conditions. Have you ever found money? Perhaps cash or coins fell out of someone's pocket, at that point, it does not have an owner unless you attempt to find that person or entity. We may lay claim to the money as ours. "Finders, keepers," as the old saying goes. Money always has an owner, and they decide the flow of money unless legal implications dictate otherwise. We must then understand our financial intentions when loaning and gifting our cash. We have discussed the perimeters of loaning money, but it is equally important to understand what gifting money means. Investopedia says, "A gift is an offering of money or assets made by one person to another in which nothing of comparable value is given, or expected to be given, in return." There we have it. The giver of the money gets nothing back, no asset, no service, and not even the money. We may be a person who has a big heart and donates to worthy causes. Oxford dictionary defines philanthropy as "The desire to promote the welfare of others, expressed especially by the generous donation of money to good causes."[6] There should then be a clear understanding of cash transfers between two parties. Sometimes in our lives, we help someone financially, typically a family member or close friend. In times of national disasters, strangers have donated money and other assets to help communities in need. Donations for Hurricane Katrina passed the $1 billion mark back in 2005.[7] These efforts warm our hearts.

There are money customs where cash is a common gift, such as a wedding, graduation, a new baby, and a new home. Most of us don't think twice about slipping $10 -$100 or more into a card as a gift to cheer someone on. This feels good, and we expect nothing in return, although a word of gratitude is appreciated. When my son graduated college, I gave him and my daughter, who had graduated two years prior, $500 in stocks. I am not sure either of them understood the value of the gift. I should have included some financial advice in conjunction with that investment to give them an investing foundation. My vision was this investment would multiply over time and be the seedlings of a nest egg well into their adult lives. The point here is to give age-appropriate gifts and not lament if the recipient blows the money. Young people receiving large sums of money collectively without a financial game plan can lead to no money left after spending sprees. Remember, expect nothing in return when you gift money.

Let's talk about bailing someone out. I mean, posting bail! How many people have been reimbursed that money gift to bail out a friend or family member? What about legal fees to assist a family member or friend? A co-worker of mine used his $30,000 401K to shave off a twenty-year sentence down to ten years for his daughter. This was his retirement, yet he gave it all for the love of his daughter.

Expect nothing in return when you gift money.

On the other hand, I have heard horror stories of the receiver of money interpreting the cash as a gift and the giver stating the money was a loan. Consider the landmark case of Mary Bolles, a mother of five who loaned money to her kids. At some point, the question became, was it a gift or a loan? Mary asserted that approximately $1.06 million were loans to her son Peter to help with his business ventures. In the end, the court split the money to the tune of $425,000 as loans.[8] Have you ever been in a position where there was a debate over loaning money, and was never repaid the money in full because your good deeds were perceived as gifts? One year my husband and I gifted $500 for school supplies to a family member with five kids. We knew they needed help, and we were in the financial position to assist. The family never asked us for money, and they were shocked when the check came in the mail. It's a good feeling when you give without receiving anything in return. Always make sure you can afford the financial gift and never expect it back when you come short of cash. The financial gift does not always have to be a large sum. Years ago, we took note of a family, husband, wife and two elementary-age kids who ran on hard times financially. They were living with his mother, so that was a big help. We purchased a nice greeting card and slipped a $50 dollar bill inside for groceries. We could hear their tears, when they called to thank us.

> It's a good feeling when you give without receiving anything in return.

I am grateful when money has been gifted to me when I have a genuine need. Years back, I became a single parent to two preteen kids after being newly divorced. My income went from a two-income household to one. Kids go through tremendous growth spurts around the preteen years, and I felt the crunch regarding shoes and clothes. The cost of school supplies for two was high, and I sometimes wondered if the school list was for my kids or the entire classroom. I was financially anxious about taking my kid's school shopping for clothes. My sister sent me a check for $200 unconditionally to bail me out and provide for my kids. Of course, I shared with my kids that their aunt was helping them with school clothes. I wanted to teach them gratitude and appreciation.

"Go-Fund-Me" accounts allow donations for people going through financial hardship. New accounts are established daily to cover funeral expenses, medical costs for accidents and hospitalizations, therapies, saving homes, and other financial needs. I have contributed multiple times to help family, friends, and others. We lost a family member unexpectedly who did not have life insurance. I never thought something like this would happen in our family. The outpouring of love and support allowed for a beautiful memorial service, headstone, and dignity for our loved one. I want to express our love and gratitude again for all the contributions, money, emotional support, and kindness.

There are tax rules regarding the specific threshold of gifting and this should be discussed with your tax advisor. According to an article in the U.S. News entitled, *Tax Rules to Know if You Give or Receive Cash*, "In 2022, gifts of up to $16,000 can be given without any tax or reporting requirements. The $16,000 threshold is one person to one person."[9] This is referring to reporting the money gift. If there is a tax implication, the giver is responsible. The Internal Revenue Service (IRS) will hold you accountable if you violate the tax reporting laws, whether you are aware of the rules or not. Make certain to consult with a tax professional.

What about giving money to a friend or family member to hold until your circumstances change? Perhaps you are going through a legal battle and don't want the money disclosed, or maybe you are trying to save money and do not trust yourself. The old saying is that "possession is 9/10ths of the law." Simple words but ones that ring true when the person you trusted has a mindset change and doesn't want to give the money back. This can be a difficult battle to fight. A family member was buying a home and couldn't qualify for credit. They put a sizable amount of money in their adult son's bank account so the son could be eligible to purchase the home with the intent that the son would quickly deed the home over to the parent once the sale closed. What do you think happened? The son began enjoying the home and reverted on the verbal agreement stating that the parent had gifted the money to him to buy a house. This created the worst family rift ever. For a time, parent and son never spoke. Over time, the son agreed to pay the money back to the parent but kept the home. How sad. Be careful with verbal agreements and putting cash in someone's hand, including family and friends.

There is a strange phenomenon that happens with money and people. Cold hard cash can make or break relationships. Couples will marry for money and divorce over it. Families will give every penny to save a loved one's life. Communities will band together to raise money for a cause, and there is no end to non-profit organizations for humanitarian efforts. Be wise about handling your money for the greater good. Put measures in place to protect yourself financially and avoid ambiguity between loaning and gifting money. We can never go wrong with expressing love and reaching out to help others when we are in a financial position to do so.

Couples will marry for money and divorce over it.

CHAPTER TEN

SHARED ACCOUNTS

When a couple weds, one of the first items on the marital to-do list is to set up joint bank accounts. This action seems to solidify their promise to love until "death do they part." I speak from experience as I followed the cookie-cutter life as my parents did by yoking our financial accounts as husband and wife. What should we know about the pros and cons of shared accounts? There are ten pros and cons to joint bank accounts according to the online publication, *Money Smart Guides*, September 10, 2021:

Pros

- Easier To Manage Finances

- Brings You Together

- Easier To Pay Bills

- Fewer Possible Fees

- Simple Legal Process

Cons

- Buying Gifts
- Money Fights
- Lack of Control
- End of the Relationship Issues
- Perceived Lack of Freedom[10]

Sharing bank accounts can become complicated as the nature of the relationship changes over time. Shared bank accounts are not limited to husbands and wives. Anyone, friends, parents, and siblings can share bank accounts. We should examine the reason for the sharing, the controls over the funds, and best-and-worst-case outcomes. Consult an attorney to understand your state's laws and the financial institution's terms and conditions.

Before filing for a divorce, I sought legal counsel to understand my financial rights. I was working full-time, and we had a profitable family business. We always carried a six-figure balance in our business account and had a generous savings account. Before filing, the attorney advised me to take out as much as I wanted from our joint account. This advice felt awkward because although the marriage was declining, I had never withdrawn large sums of money without a discussion and mutual agreement. Remember the old saying I mentioned earlier "possession is 9/10ths of the law?" I first heard that adage from the mouth of my attorney. How could I do something like this? It felt like financial cheating. The attorney reminded me that my husband could do the same to me, take the money, and run before I got to it. I couldn't do it. A year later, I filed for a divorce, and I kept all the money intact, and so did he, and we did the right thing by splitting the funds per the courts. I do know of a co-worker who had a different outcome. She came home from work one day to an empty house, and the bank account drained of approximately $20,000. Her husband left her and would later serve her with divorce papers. She never got that money back. This can be rather difficult when you assume you can trust the other party.

I got a wake-up call when I learned about a term called *relationship banking* when I was going through a divorce. My husband and I had our mortgage account, our children's individual savings account, and a business account at the same bank. I opened a separate checking and savings account at another bank as we began to divide our money during the divorce process. We owned two homes, meaning he was paying for his home at the bank with our kids' accounts, and I was making my mortgage payment to a different lender. My husband missed two mortgage payments, and the bank took the money out of our children's savings account. I was devastated, confused, and angry. Not angry at my ex-husband as he was unaware of the bank's actions. I called the bank's branch manager, and he informed me that the bank had a legal right to withdraw the past due mortgage payments due to the parent-child relationship. Of course, I immediately closed those accounts and opened new accounts at my new bank. My husband did repay the money in the financial settlement of our divorce.

A significant financial risk exposure if one of the joint bank account holders has a legal garnishment order. A distant relative had his two adult children in his bank account, which always carried a six-figure balance. The daughter had a foreclosure from a past property that she thought was resolved as the home returned to the bank. The father received a notice from the bank that $100,000 was withdrawn from his account in compliance with a court order to settle a foreclosure for his daughter. The entire family was in shock and upset. The father was weak as this was his funds accumulated from his monthly social security benefits and pension. The bank's hands were tied as they had to comply with the legal order. The daughter hired an attorney to attempt to recover the money. The opposing party's legal counsel fought just as hard to retain the money. The legal expenses amounted to $5,000 for the daughter. The father added his children to his account as a precaution should something happen to him. He has since listed the two children as beneficiaries only of his account. The judge ruled in favor of the daughter because the father's account was a social security income account, and the daughter had never deposited or withdrawn money from that account. The father could have suffered a great financial loss if the outcome had been different. We can learn a lot from these life lessons. Consult with an attorney for more clarification on your state's laws and the financial institutions' terms and conditions.

In other instances, you may financially obligate yourself regarding credit cards and a spouse. Even when our family business flourished, I had always earned income in a corporate career position. We had two children, a home, and two vehicles, and we loved to take family vacations. Before marriage, I had multiple credit cards with an average of $10,000 per card credit limit. As you can imagine, it was easy to rack up credit card charges as a family for dining, traveling, kid things, and who knows what else. I had become overconfident about our income; before I knew it, I had racked up $10,000 in credit card balances. This would be equivalent to $17,579 in 2022. Why are we discussing credit card balances? Once my husband found out, he demanded I pay every penny of the $10,000 out of my paycheck! I remember sobbing about these circumstances that, in my opinion, were not all my debt. After all, I had charged things for the family, including the kids and the hubby. I caved in and took out a twelve-month $10,000 loan against my 401K. I was paid every two weeks, and with this new loan, $900 a month was deducted from my paycheck. I was crushed emotionally and financially because although we had shared income bank accounts, my paycheck was still being depleted. There was no room for me to divert other money to my company credit union or other accounts such as savings. I am not sure why I had to pay this money back. Word to the wise, be careful how you use your credit and for whom you charge. You are legally obliged to make monthly payments until the balance is paid in full. Also, bear in mind the interest rates on the charges if not paid in full each month. Look at the payoff charges included on the credit card statements, to see how much you will have paid over the years on your balances. As a financial coach, I help clients find strategies to pay off credit card balances, grow their money, and set up for future income.

Be mindful of allowing other people to possess your credit card if they are not listed as authorized users. A friend asked if I would loan her and her business partner $30,000 dollars for three months with interest. They needed the money to start a project and had a contract to prove to me they could repay my loan. Here I go again, pretending to be a banker. I agreed to allow them to use two of my credit cards, and I drew $5,000 cash from a credit line I had at the bank. We are talking twenty years ago when I was naive and financially illiterate. They agreed to pay me back, including interest charges incurred on the credit line and the credit cards. We signed a promissory note, and I felt good about it all. Three months came and went, and I had not been paid. How do you ask for your money? These are friends, and they know they owe me. I sent communication reminders and finally worked up the nerve to call and talk to them about it. Of course, I was told they had delayed payments from their client. The problem is that I was making the monthly payments on the credit line and credit cards, of which they agreed to pay all of that back. My neck was on the line financially, and if they never paid me a dime, there would be nothing I could do about it. I was sweating and crying simultaneously as I realized I could get stuck if they defaulted. Eventually, the client paid my friends, and they paid me. Things got a little weird when they looked at paying finance charges. Somehow, they couldn't remember agreeing to pay for that, but they did so reluctantly to keep the peace. This was a gross misuse of my credit card. I was incurring monthly expenses that were not mine, which put a huge dent in my cash flow for months.

Be a good steward of your money and understand the rules of the financial road. Money and emotions don't make a good mix. It's so easy to accept money but hard to give back when terms and conditions apply. Show respect for your money and your relationships. Don't presume upon people's money. Some say, "He or she has the money; they can afford it." It's not for us to determine whether someone can afford something financially. Be careful of "getting rich" quick offers. If it sounds too good to be true, it usually is not good or true. Always consult with attorneys, tax pros, and financial professionals.

> It's so easy to accept money but hard to give back when terms and conditions apply.

Money, Family, and Friends

THE FLOW
OF MONEY

The Flow of Money

All for One and One for All

Flashing Cash

Distinction of Money

Money Destroys

CHAPTER ELEVEN

THE FLOW OF MONEY

When we think of the word *flow*, we may envision a continuous movement or stream of something like water out of a facet. Money or currency movement flows through societies and is the basis for conducting commerce, governmental tax regulations and standard of living thresholds. Money comes in various forms, such as paper, coins, cryptocurrency and NFTs. The purpose of the US dollar bill took on a new meaning in 1861 when it was printed to finance the Civil War. Coins of differing metals were then and still are being used worldwide as an accepted means of exchange. How do we maximize the flow of money? For some people, money comes in abundance for others, its scarcity can

> How does money make you feel when you see or smell it?

be life-altering. Let's examine for a minute our relationship with money and how this can significantly impact how money does or does not flow in our lives to our satisfaction.

How does money make you feel when you see or smell it? In the United States, for example, the color of the dollar bill is green. Initially, the color green was selected as a deterrent to counterfeiting because of the copy limitation of black-and-white photography. In the mid-1900s, green was associated with stability, according to History.com's article *Why is American Currency Green?*[11] Today there are abundant resources that relate green to prosperity, abundance, safety, harmony and nature. Some see green in a negative light. Have you heard this term, *green with envy*? Some people perceive the color green as drawing jealousy, greed and possessiveness.

Imagine having these negative vibes about green and wondering why you are not attracting money. In the financial world, the color green is used in graphs, charts, and illustrations to show gains, growth and profits. Green may be a part of brand colors for financial institutions, banks and investment organizations. Since becoming a financial coach, I have added the color green to my wardrobe. The only time I wore green was during my high school years when our student body was called the "Green Wave." Green was never a color of choice until I started learning about the money flow and getting my financial coaching license. Now, I look for green dresses, pants, tops and accessories whenever I shop. Why am I sharing this with you? My perception and understanding of money changed. I began to feel more comfortable speaking about money and how I can increase its flow in my life and educate communities and households to do the same. I recently attended a women's event, and the question was asked, "Share about your favorite color, like green." There was a subtle message with this question. We were at tables of eight, and I was the only person who said green was my favorite color. Everyone else named various colors. When this question was read aloud by the event organizer, only a few people in the room of approximately seventy people, all women, stated that green was their favorite color. The event organizer stated, "Green should be everyone's favorite color because it's the color of money!" Every woman in the room cheered and applauded. This was a great lesson on picking up on the money vibes and allowing the flow in our thought processes. Your feelings about money can play an important role in the flow of money in your life. Are you repelling money?

Often, our perception of money flowing manifests in how we move about in society. Do you disparage others who have money in abundance because of your feelings? Are you a giver or a taker when it comes to money? Have you heard the term "tightwad?" This phase implies that a person holds on tight to their money. This person feels uncomfortable with money flowing without a specific need and may have a good sense of discount pricing and budget spending.

On the other spectrum, there is the person that splurges and shells out money frivolously. I have been out on a ladies' shopping day, and let me tell you, some of us were buying on the emotional side of spending and walking out with bags and bags of things. We would later go home and rejoice as we pulled out our items with pride and joy. This is happy spending of your money flow but should not be wasteful. Make sure you can afford this flow and have allotted a spending day in your financial budget. Some people are referred to as money hungry and are always trying to make a buck regardless of the risk to themselves or others. Still, others can't seem to hold on their cash. Some money habits may stem from how we were raised and the examples set by our parents or role models (good or bad). Who recalls these words, "A penny saved, is a penny earned," by Benjamin Franklin? I have seen people discard and throw pennies away. The Readers Digest reported an interesting fact about loose change and coins in an article entitled *Your Change Makes the TSA Wealthier: Change Adds up Fast.* In 2015, the TSA reported collecting $765,759.15 in loose change at airport security checkpoints across the country.[12] They get to keep it all. Does this make you rethink your money flow when it comes to those loose coins in your purse, kitchen table, or pocket? Time to get that penny jar started again. This also makes me wonder what happens to the coins tossed in public fountains. Where does that money go? It's time to rethink throwing money away. Generational money flow habits start early. Parents let's teach our children to save those coins rather than toss them.

We must form a balanced and healthy view of the flow of money. Have you heard it said, "Money is the root of all evil" or "The love of money is the root of evil?" Why would one associate evil with money? These words may give way to some people who choose ill-begotten gain to attain money, perhaps by lying, stealing or cheating. These actions don't make money itself bad but rather refer to the disdain of the deceitful methods used to covet financial gain. For three months, I hosted a series entitled *Love, Family & Finances 2022,* in which I had experts speak on several topics. One wealth and money coach stated that we must fall in love with money in a good way, like a friendship with someone close and trusted. The term money monster is used when some people fear money and find themselves repelling it. Can you see the picture in your mind? Think of this: if you are afraid to check your bank balance, you fear money. People who embrace the money flow and focus on saving and growing their money are eager to review their account balances. This is a healthy love of money, not to be confused with greed or an imbalanced view of financial gain.

> We must fall in love with money in a good way, like a friendship with someone close and trusted.

As a financial coach, I educate and empower communities to become comfortable talking about their money flow. What are your spending habits? Do you have an emergency fund or a saving account? Do you have a sufficient household operating account? A budget is one of the best tools we can use to manage the money flow. This is more than accounting for our daily, weekly and monthly money flow. Tracking our income and expenses is a great way to find holes in our money bucket where money could be pouring out. My husband and I found $400 a month on eating out for breakfast every day. We soon ended this frivolous cycle once we captured this expense. We now treat ourselves to eating breakfast occasionally, and it feels special when we do. Breakfast food is one of the cheapest meals, and keeping these foods on tap at home is easy. Another money flow habit for me was to stop window shopping for clothes. My pastime would be a stroll in the mall or department stores for a mental break, but I always came out with a bag of something I did not need. Grocery shopping should be intentional and planned. We broke the habit of making multiple trips to pick up one or two items, which always resulted in bringing home extra items not needed for the week. Do you see how money flows manifest in your daily life? Pay more attention to when and how often money leaves your hands. How do you feel when you spend money or increase your bank account? There are plenty of free budget tools online, or you can create your own excel spreadsheet at home. Keep this process simple. Set up a bowl or jar at home for receipts to be recorded on your spreadsheet. Get the family to buy in by offering a reward when you start seeing savings from your tracking. Respect your money, and yes, count your coins.

> Pay more attention to when and how often money leaves your hands.

CHAPTER TWELVE

ALL FOR ONE AND ONE FOR ALL

Who gets the spoils, the gold, and yes, the money when it comes down to divvying up assets? The Three Musketeers were community do-gooders, working for the good of the whole. Team, friend, soulmate and best friend can quickly transition into the singular word "I" when money is at stake. Have you heard the expression, "Money unmasks people?" Then, there are true-blue, loyal-to-the-end relationships where money holds no value to the bond of the relationship. The adage "he/she will give you the shirt off his/her back" tells you that this person is a giver, not a receiver. How do we size this up in finance, family and friends? We are speaking of financial assets and the rules of access, touching, managing, sharing and controlling.

One of the most overlooked asset management accounts is one's 401k company-sponsored plan. I was excited to work for a company with benefits, which included a 401k matching plan. Participating in this type of plan is a great opportunity to get free money from your employer via their matching program. When you enroll in this program, you must list beneficiaries and your spouse's information if you are married. According to my company plan, my spouse was entitled to 100% of my 401k or a lesser percentage that I determined with his consent in combination with other beneficiaries I named. I also had to get his signature if I wanted to change my plan. This is all well and good when the relationship is positive. This plan's transparency can be tough if the relationship is not good. It can be a very sticky situation, and I know because it happened to me when I was going through my divorce. When we were good, it was our money, even though I contributed from my paycheck. We had family plans. As the relationship started deteriorating, I realized he had some entitlement. I did not want to share, and he wanted every penny he was entitled to by law. This was the hardest financial pill that I ever had to swallow in my life. With over twenty-five years of contributions, legally, I had to fork over half of my pension and 401k funds.

My mother said, "Sabrina, it's only money, and you will get it all back one day." Ten years later, I had grown my funds back up, but I lost the growth I would have had. Understand the laws and your money. We can't go around the law, but perhaps you can work out some financial settlements that are mutually beneficial to all. I know of some couples who did not split up the 401k but bartered other assets like a greater portion of the profits from the sale of a home or granting a full financial right to a family business instead of company-sponsored funds.

> Sabrina, it's only money, and you will get it all back one day.

These are true stories for educational purposes and shouldn't be construed as legal advice. Always consult with a tax and legal professional for advisement.

Your money is my money, and my money is my money can happen in some household relationships. I worked full-time, and my first husband started a family business during our marriage. We both had equal control and access to my income, while I had limited control over the income profits of his business. My first husband purchased a van without my knowledge, with money from the business. On the other hand, I was riding around in a hot car because the air conditioning had gone out. My husband told me that we couldn't afford to buy me a new car even though we had cash in our joint checking and saving accounts and I had my 401k, and I earned enough income to afford a car payment. His money was his money, and my money was our money. Eventually, I took out a loan from my 40lk and paid cash for a car without his knowledge. He was not happy with me at the time as I had made a financial decision about my 401k, even though he had done the same with the business funds. This was a very unbalanced financial relationship, and scenarios like this would continue. On another occasion, he came home with a $2500 big-screen TV for our home entertainment, which caught me by surprise.

However, I couldn't spend more than $100 on anything without consulting with him. This may sound like control, but it was a matter of understanding how money works in relationships and setting up financial rules and boundaries at the onset. We could have benefited from working with a financial coach and setting up a financial game plan that included mutual budgeting and asset management.

There are tools we can utilize that offer financial protection for couples before they wed. As mentioned, engage a financial coach or advisor to help map your goals. In the case of a pending marriage, a prenuptial (prenup) agreement may be a way to ensure asset protection for both parties. The dictionary defines a prenup as an agreement made by a couple before they marry concerning the ownership of their respective assets should the marriage fail. I have heard horror stories where one mate was drained financially of assets resulting from a divorce. Opening a conversation between love birds about signing a pre-up can be awkward. One person may feel their honesty and integrity are being questioned. "But, I love you, I would never take advantage of you" is often the initial knee-jerk response to the subject matter of a prenup. The mind can't think about love and divorce simultaneously in terms of financial planning. Pre-ups are not just for wealthy couples. Couples of modest means could benefit as well. There are eight reasons to consider setting up a prenup, according to PrenuptualAgreements.org:

- You are much wealthier than your partner

- You earn much more money than your partner

- You are remarrying

- Your partner has a high debt load

- You own part of a business

- To prevent your spouse from overturning your estate plan

- You have less money than your spouse

- If you plan to quit your job and raise children[13]

Prenups can address child support, debt protection, family heirlooms, real estate, and premarital assets. What did I do when I married my second husband? We signed a prenup. The conversations were uncomfortable for both of us, but in the end, we both knew this was the right thing to do. Years into our marriage, the prenup document rarely comes up in conversation. This is peace of mind that both mates should have. If you can't have that financial conversation before marriage, it will be even tougher after the marriage, should a divorce occur. What can you do now if you desire to implement this type of agreement and are already married? A postnuptial agreement is a document for couples to decide how to split assets—these agreements are not DIY (do it yourself) documents. You must consult with an attorney in both a prenup and a post-nup for these legal agreements/contracts.

Let's talk about children and who manages and controls household assets. There are many different family dynamics these days due to blended families. There are no guidelines or set rules as each family and relationship is different. There may be cases of an inheritance or sizable bank account for a minor child. I recall a mother who had passed away and left beneficiary money to her minor child, who, was now in the care of the father and remarried. Who controls and manages these funds? What was the will of the deceased mother? These are very sensitive matters, and it would be wise to seek the advisement of a legal professional. A wife or husband may get child support for her/his biological child/children that only she/he controls. I have seen cases where this money is kept separate and used to care for the children's basic needs in the new marriage. In other cases, the wife (or husband) may choose to blend that money into the household accounts for general use for the entire family. This should be discussed and mutually agreed upon by both mates. Keep the lines of financial communication open to ensure no misunderstanding or ambiguity. As a financial coach, I work with couples to ensure that all income and expenditures are accounted for and are planned properly for the best possible financial outcome for the household.

CHAPTER THIRTEEN

FLASHING CASH

There was a time when people would walk around with wads of cash in their pockets or purses. There was a sense of security when we had money at our fingertips for whatever may come our way during the day. Times have changed to a certain degree with the creation of debit and credit cards. Endless apps are available to us to transfer funds with a few clicks. Some people still live by the physical currency of cash and coins and would never leave home without it. How do you feel when you carry cash? Do you have a threshold on the amount of cash you carry? Have you been inside a bank lately? We have drive-through banking services with videos of your interaction with the teller. Yet the circulation of U.S. currency is strong. According to an article on www.History.com, there is $1.2 trillion in coins and paper money in circulation in America.[14] Our money is still moving, being transferred from hand to hand and institution to institution. How do you handle cash?

Bank tellers, retailers, and anyone working with cash are taught to count money out when receiving and dispensing. We can appreciate our math teachers who taught us how to count money. Even with technology where change is displayed on a terminal or register, the employee may still be required to count your currency in plain sight.

There are endless stories of customers claiming shortages or even employees receiving the cash having drawer deficiencies. These same situations can happen to friends and families. My brother was selling a stereo system to my husband many years ago for $200. The money was folded in half as my husband handed the wad to my brother. Once my brother got home, he counted the cash and was short. Talk about an uncomfortable family situation. What do you think happened? We had to give my brother the shortage even though my husband stood his ground that all of the cash was there. My brother did not feel the need to count the money because a wad of cash looks good but can be deceiving. Another relative was good at bookkeeping and was entrusted to make deposits for a local church. A church member gave her $1,000 in cash folded up to take to the bank. She never counted the money because she wanted it to stay intact. The bank teller counted $700! She was very upset because her honor was at stake. The church member denied the shortage, and the church took the financial hit. These things happen in business as well. A family member had a service-related business in which a client went to his home for a part. The client handed a wad of cash to the business owner's spouse, not counted out. The promised $1,400 turned out to be $1,000 the business owner received the money. Do you accuse the client or the spouse of the shortage? This was a very dicey situation. All of this could have been avoided by counting money.

> We can appreciate our math teachers who taught us how to count money.

The business owner took the hit as the spouse and client denied they shorted the cash. Recently, a family member was selling some products to a friend. There was a miscommunication on the product cost as the friend gave folded-up cash for one item, not two items. The family member gave two items and never counted the cash until they arrived home. They had to decide whether to pay for the second item or return it. This made for a very tense conversation and reluctance to do business again for both parties. The moral of these real-life stories is to count your money at all times regardless of the receiver or the giver.

When we consider paying with money, often, we think of dollar bills. In centuries past, coins were acceptable methods of currency for daily living. When was the last time you saw someone pay for a big-ticket item with coins? We are talking about flashing cash, but what about coins? Some people save coins as a means to pay for things. I was dating a guy once who defaulted to his sock of coins when his bank account was low. We met at a local high-end restaurant, where we asked for separate checks. I whipped out my debit card, and he pulled out his sock of coins. You should have seen the look on the waiter's face, dude are you kidding? My date was not fazed by this look, as his coins were sufficient to cover his bill. I later heard that this was the talk of the staff. My guy friend apparently was not the only person to pay for his meal with coins.

A teen waiter saved up his tip money, mostly coins, to treat his friends to a meal and was shamed on social media, according to Today.com. According to the article, the teen's check amounted to $45 plus a $10 tip. This experience begs the question, are coins acceptable for leaving tips? When is the last time you left coins for your server? There was an article in the Huffington Post about a man who paid the DMV (Department of Motor Vehicles) $2,978.14 for a tax bill with 298,745 pennies. It took the staff approximately 24 hours to count the 1,548 pounds of change by hand. This is an extreme case; however, some people live by the coin.

We are in a new age of paying on the spot with apps such as Cash App, Venmo, Zelle, PayPal, Square and countless others. Be mindful that there are fees attached to some of these transactions that may seem small but add up. For example, let's assume the transfer fee is 3% when you send $30 to someone; this transaction cost is only .90 cents. This seems minimal; however, this could easily add up to $9.00 if you did this same amount ten times or the transfer amount was $300. In some cases, the transfer fee is passed on to the business and not the customer if this is a business transaction. Ensure that you have done your due diligence in selecting a safe and secure money transaction service. A girlfriend of mine sold some furniture she advertised publicly and accepted a cash app form of payment on the spot. She did not accept the payment right away. Sometime later, she checked the payment, and it had been reversed! The buyer drove off with the furniture and rescinded the payment. My friend recovered her payment by threatening legal action against the buyers. Years ago, a co-worker sold her ATV (All-Terrain Vehicle) to a stranger for $900. The man flashed $200 cash and offered a check for the remaining $700. My co-worker accepted the deal. The check bounced, and my co-worker never saw the man again. Check scams were very common back in the day, from buying a big-ticket item to paying for your groceries. Checks can be electronically verified before you leave the place of business. You may ask, who still writes checks? My mother does.

ATMs (automatic teller machines) have become a common resource for getting cash in hand quickly. It's almost too easy to get your hands on your money. In our early years of marriage, my husband and I were hitting up the ATM several times a week for $20 each. This added up to approximately $160 a week. This was a budget killer as we were being wasteful. One time the machine kept my card and did not dispense the cash as the account was overdrawn. I was unaware of what hubby had taken out and vice versa. This was a big wake-up call for both of us. We were not good stewards of our money. We set ATM rules, and that never happened again. Word to the wise, some ATMs will assess a fee to non-banking customers. Count the cost of your withdrawals. Sometimes the fees are small compared to the cost of fuel to drive to your banking institution and your time. There is also the issue of safety when using an ATM in dark or secluded areas.

Think twice about how you handle money, whether receiving or giving. Be on the lookout for counterfeit money. A friend of mine was paying for gas inside the store, and before he and his wife could exit the store, the police confronted them. The cashier reported the $100 bill that my friend was using to pay for his fuel as fake. My friend had received this bill from another transaction that he had made. The end of the story is that he did not go to jail, but he was out $100. The United States Department of Treasury reports an estimated $70 -$200 million in counterfeit bills are in circulation at any given time. The $20 bill is the most counterfeited note reported by Reuters. When we think of flashing cash, be aware that all money is not good.

CHAPTER FOURTEEN

DISTINCTION OF MONEY

The abundance of money or the lack of the green United States currency can create economic class distinction. In the United States, there are six different socio-economic classes, as reported by William Thompson & Joseph Hickey, 2005:

- **Upper Class (1%)**

  $500,000+ Income

- **Upper Middle Class (15%)**

  $100,000 or High 5 figure Income

- **Lower Middle Class (32%)**

  $35,000 - $75,000

- **Working Class (32%)**

  $16,000 – $30,000

- **Lower Class (20%)**

  Below numbers above[15]

These categories don't reflect one's intellect, values, or abilities. Often we find ourselves spending close to the money we earn. We may live in an earn-spend cycle. If that is the case, all of the aforementioned class distinctions may have the same concern, the need for more money. We may find ourselves trying to keep up with the Joneses and burning through our hard-earned cash.

Where and how we live may give the impression of the amount of cash at our fingertips. One of my favorite movies of all time is *Home Alone*. While it's a comedy, the premise of the story is that the thieves chose a wealthy neighborhood to do their dirty deeds of robbery. It's the look of money that lures and attracts for good or bad. A round of applause to those who are managing their financial portfolio to have the lifestyle they desire. We don't want to live above our means to look like we have more assets than we do. There are endless stories of people pretending to be wealthy and taking advantage of others for material gain.

In the United States, a fancy foreign car seems to give the impression of wealth. I have seen men and women date a person based on the car they drive without knowing much else about the person. About eight years ago, I purchased an economy car because I did not want to be a slave to the rising fuel cost. I love my car and still have it. When I rolled up to a girlfriend's home with my new car, she said, "That's it? That's what you bought?" She went on to say that she expected me to ride up in a Cadillac or Mercedes Benz. I went for comfort and economy and still stand by that. I love Cadillacs and Mercedes Benz and may own one of these vehicles one day as my second or third car. The message in this story is how money can create distinction. She knew me as a businesswoman and expected me to show my money by vehicle.

Some people use their cash or perceived cash to buy relationships and attention. Have you ever been around a guy or woman who never allows you to forget how much money he or she makes or has? Maybe they pay for everything, or maybe they don't. Or what about the person that makes you feel like they are always short on cash? When I was single, a group of friends routinely went out to dinner to wind down from the week. There was this one person who would show up broke, even to the point of ordering only water. Of course, we would always chip in so this individual could eat a hot meal. This person, we found out later, was earning a decent salary with a nice standard of living. Of course, the gravy train came to a complete stop. Then there is the person who always pulls out big bills in front of everyone to pay for things. I went to dinner with a couple, and just before the check arrived, he had to leave, but he reassured me he would cover the entire check, which I was not expecting. He pulled out several $100 bills and plopped one on the table for me to pay for the meal. My first thought was, who walks around with that kind of money on them? I may be a little old-fashioned, but I don't carry cash like that on me, let alone showcase it for others to see. I am sure my feelings have much to do with my upbringing and money culture. I am always thinking about safety as well. As mentioned earlier, on the rare occasion I did have a large sum of money, I felt like everyone I walked past knew I was carrying money. I couldn't wait to unload the money at its final destination, in most cases, the bank.

Sometimes people are sought out for their money and become prey to shady business deals and shallow romantic relationships. Have you heard the term "gold digger?" The dictionary defines Gold Digger as: "A person who forms a relationship with another purely to extract money from them." It's hard for millionaires and billionaires to hide their net worth from the general public. If possible, I encourage you to keep your net worth private to fend off predators. Even on the simplest of applications, due to credit score evaluations, real estate investments, and other financial portfolio items disclosure of one's network may be required. However, we can do our due diligence and thoroughly check out strangers that pop up out of nowhere and want to enter our warm circle. Background checks don't cost much and could be a wise investment to save a lot of pain, heartache, and even financial ruin at the hands of a devious person.

Sometimes we undervalue a person because of their outward appearance. A while back, my husband and I walked into a Volkswagen showroom to purchase the car of our dreams at the time. We had seen this cute little Volkswagen Jetta that was the talk of the town then. The salesman seemed to size us up immediately and started showing us pre-owned low-ticket Volkswagen Beetles and Bugs. That was not what we wanted. We wanted the Jetta. We left that dealership and drove to another city because of the stereotypical customer service. There it was, sitting in the showroom, the Jetta, nice and shining. Sunroof top, leather seats, seat warmers, and all the bells and whistles. This salesperson treated us like we could have whatever we wanted. For the first time, I drove a car out of the showroom. We took that baby home. We were a two-income household with no kids and no debt at the time.

There are countless stories of famous people who dress down so they can blend in with crowds to avoid raving fans, according to an article on The Richest.com: *15 of The Richest People In the World (Who Look Like They're Poor).*[16] These billionaires enjoy wearing regular jeans, t-shirts, and boots. You will see them shopping in discount stores, neighborhood coffee shops, and fast-food drive-throughs.

As a financial coach, I focus on your money, working for and rewarding you. There is nothing wrong with wearing designer attire and having the life of the rich and famous as long as your bank account supports your lifestyle. Be mindful of trying to give the appearance of a lifestyle beyond your means. You may rob yourself of a secure financial future with unnecessary overspending and mounting debt.

Count the cost of where and how you spend your money. Always evaluate your ROI (Return On Investment). This applies to every aspect of our lives. A membership, for example, is a financial expenditure that could be considered an investment when there are benefits. Sometimes the relationships at the club or organization are extremely valuable and worth every penny of the membership cost. Many business deals were initiated on the country club greens or local networking association. Gym memberships can be a waste of money if you are not using it regularly. We paid for an entire year of gym membership for my husband, who only went once. In his mind, he was going, but his body never did. It was that mental thing in his head to say he belonged to a gym. We did cancel the membership eventfully.

How many items do you have in your possession that you are not using but purchased it so you can claim you have it? Over time you let the item go, either as a giveaway to a friend or at a yard sale for a fraction of the price. My daughter loves to go thrifting. She is always picking up new to barely used designer items for pennies on the dollar. My words of wisdom here are to make your money work for you, think before you spend, and live the lifestyle your financial game plan supports.

> Think before you spend, and live the lifestyle your financial game plan supports.

CHAPTER FIFTEEN

MONEY DESTROYS

The lust for money can break up families, business relationships, and friendships. It is the coveting of money and wealth that feeds unthinkable destruction. A local tragic story has stuck with me for over thirty-seven years of a family in Naples, Florida. I lived in Fort Myers at the time, about thirty minutes from Naples, and I remember living through this story on TV and in our newspaper. To my surprise, the story aired in January 2021 on Oxygen True Crime: *After Setting Off Bombs In An SUV To Murder His Wealthy Family, Man Left His Sister To Burn To Death On Lawn.*[17] On August 22, 1985, the older son, Steven Benson, had lured his mother, sister, and younger adoptive brother into the family SUV (packed with explosives) to look at a property. Once they were loaded inside the vehicle, Steven went back into the home when the SUV exploded. His sister survived to tell the story. The prosecutor surmised that greed for family wealth was at the root of this crime. I wrote a college paper entitled "Truth" which covered the story of the Menendez Brothers, Lyle, and Erik, who were convicted for the 1989 murders of their parents for family money. Within six months of the parents' deaths, the boys had spent $700,000 of the father's fourteen million net worth. From hindsight to insight, we are learning the value of keeping our personal financial information away from people who don't need to know it.

Losing loved ones has caused families to break up over wills and perceived inheritance. An entire family I know has severed ties over cash disbursement from the deceased parent. They say time heals all wounds, but sometimes that does not happen. In this case, the ties remain broken even though years have passed, and I imagine all the inherited money is gone. A high school classmate sued her father over the family fortune after her mother passed away. A daughter convinced her mother to secretly sign over multiple acres of land to her. The other siblings were unaware of this deal until the mother regretted her actions. This caused a big rift with the entire family, which excluded the other sibling from getting anything if the mother passed away. The mother tried to get the daughter to rescind the deal, and she refused. The mother took her daughter to court and lost because she signed the papers of her own free will. We are getting some good money lessons on handling money with family. A son drained all the money out of his mother's life insurance policy, unbeknownst to his other siblings. When the mother passed away, the family discovered that the mother did not have a death benefit available. They had to pool together financially to bury their mom. This left a trail of broken trust in this family. This would be a great time to review life insurance policies to ensure that they are being paid, not lapsed, and that the death benefit is still intact.

There are instances where family members hide money from each other such as husbands and wives. There may be secret bank accounts, investment funds, real estate, and other assets. This may be a necessary strategy if the other person in the relationship is not trustworthy, irresponsible with money, a gambler, or have unsavory ties with others that could jeopardize the health and wealth of the family. This is not to overlook that a healthy relationship should be open, honest, and trustworthy. I encourage couples to be open and work as a financial team to reach their goals. The common thread in this book is to be a good steward of your money.

Sometimes we have to practice tough love when a family member or friend borrows money. Our human nature to help kicks in when we see someone we love in need, and we have the financial means to help. Our assistance can turn darkness into light for some who are forever grateful and repay the deed when they are back on their feet. Then there is the family member or friend who keeps returning for money multiple times for as long as you allow it. They are always short on cash and need a little help. We are not helping this person, but rather we are creating a cycle of co-dependency. The adage comes into play, feed a man a fish, and he eats for a day, teach him how to fish, and he eats for a lifetime. Saying 'no' is easier said than done when our hearts are involved. The financial principle, in this case, is to teach the person in need how to survive on their own. Perhaps steer the person to some public resources or assist them in finding income or employment. Maybe help them start a new trade, look for something they are good at, or teach them how to generate income with their natural talent.

> Sometimes we have to practice tough love when a family member or friend borrows money.

We talked earlier about relationship breakups and the financial impacts on one or both parties. There have been some public divorces settlements such as Jeff Bezos and Mackenzie Scott – $38 Billion, Tiger Woods and Elin Nordegren - $710 million, and Mel and Robyn Moore Gibson - $425 Million according to the article, *10 Most Expensive Divorce Settlements, in History* on ManofMany.com.[18] We discussed the value of putting prenups and post-nups in place that could take the financial sting out of divorces. If we are parents of young adult children, it would be wise to educate our kids on protecting their assets before their hearts get involved with another person. There is an even more critical need for this family discussion in cases where an inheritance may be in their future.

There are situations where step-families create division between biological siblings and natural parents when money is involved.

Consider this real-life story of a wife and mother who remarried when her husband passed away. The wife had several natural children, and the new husband had natural kids, but they had none together. All of the kids bonded into a nice happy family. The new husband moves into the wife's home, and a few years later, the wife passes away. The new husband takes control of the wife's money and home, which her kids thought they would get. He moves his adult kids into the home. Her kids are at war with his kids and the husband of their deceased mom. Years later, he remarries and moves his new wife into the home. If the deceased wife could have peered into the future, she may have put a financial safety net in place to protect her assets and leave a legacy for her natural children. Are you considering marriage? Consult with an attorney to discuss ways that you can preserve your estate. We will discuss a few measures in this book that can be taken later on.

> Money got in the way, other people got in the way, and sad to say, the damage was not repairable.

Money can destroy even the best of friendships. Have you seen best friends go into business, and it tore up the relationship? There are many moving parts in partnership. Daily operational decisions, managing funds, and business planning can be challenging for two people to agree on equally. Have both parties invested equally financially? Is there an operation document in place? Is there a legally enforceable partnership agreement in place? When money is at stake, love, and good faith sometimes go out the window. I know of long-time friends who treated each other like family until a business deal went sour. Being old-fashioned, they relied on a handshake and never signed papers between themselves. Money got in the way, other people got in the way, and sad to say, the damage was not repairable.

The movie *The Founder* is a great example of keeping watch over your assets and relationships. This is the story of how the food chain McDonald's was started in 1940 by two brothers, Richard, and Maurice McDonald, and then franchised in partnership with Ray

Kroc. Through a series of strategies and legal moves, the McDonald brothers lost the growth of the franchise and sold out to Ray Kroc in 1961 for 2.7 million. If the brothers had not sold out, their royalty fee would have been $305 million back in 2012, according to Mashed. com. Today the McDonald's Franchise is worth $170 billion. The McDonald brothers went on to live modest lives until their deaths. This story taught me about entrepreneurship, leadership, business, money, real estate, and financial strategies. *Hindsight to Insight* is to learn from the mistakes we make and those made by others. Engage the help of licensed and skilled professionals who offer the greatest safety net and are willing to put things in laymen's language so that you understand your circumstances and impending decisions that need to be made. Mentorship and education are important factors in business and financial game planning. Keep up to date on innovations, new processes, and products that can help you grow your assets.

Money, Family, and Friends

WEALTH
BUILDING

$

CHAPTER SIXTEEN

WEALTH BUILDING

Who wants to be a millionaire? Or should we say, who doesn't want to be a millionaire? Growing up, we never heard the word wealth in our home or social environment. We would refer to someone who seemed to have it all as being rich. As kids, we dreamed of being rich, which meant owning assets with no accountability. This mindset spilled over into my adult life as I never connected the dots about what wealth meant in today's terms. The definition of wealth can be very personalized based on our value system and level of contentment. The Merriam-Webster dictionary defines wealth as "Abundant material possessions or resources."[19] How do we know when we have met our plentiful threshold? The answer is simple, we have met or exceeded our financial game plan of assets.

The building aspect implies a continuous movement of combining multiple things to achieve a finished product. Wealth building is an abundance of our combined assets growing into our desired financial masterpiece. This financial crescendo involves planning, time, months, and years of defining, fine-tuning, gains and losses, learning, reading, seeking mentorship, and staying alert to innovation, technology, world news and events. The good news is that you don't have to have a surplus of money or assets to start this long-term process. The greatest success can be acquired when establishing and implementing a wealth-building plan as early as possible. I would suggest that when a person is old enough to save money, meaning young people, that is the best time to start planning how to make it work short and long-term. Some people, youth and adults, get too focused on saving to spend rather than saving to grow into wealth for sustainable financial security.

> Some get too focused on saving to spend rather than saving to grow into wealth.

WEALTH-BUILDING PROCESS

Earning money

Creating cash flow is the first step in the wealth-building process. This could be getting a job or starting a business. New businesses are started every day, which is a great time to start wealth building. "Pay yourself first" is a principle in many business coaching programs.

Income Generation

Multiple income streams (passive) are the next level of increasing your cash flow. The more money you make, the more you have to work with for wealth building.

Stash The Cash

Saving money is the next step in the wealth-building process. We must be coachable when it comes to setting money aside. Small savings turn into big savings, and big savings turn into massive savings. Out of sight, out of mind works for some people, while others want to see their money regularly. Even with debt, it may be possible to save some money.

Putting Your Money to Work

Growing assets and turning money into more money is called investing. They are various types of investing with varying degrees of risk from high to low. A broad range of money growth options should be discussed with a financial professional.

Wealth building goes hand in hand with building a safe and sturdy financial house. Wealth building is not acquiring things that will not appreciate or grow. A good example of wealth-building blockers is items that will depreciate. Purchasing a car, a boat, extravagant attire, luxury vacations, costume jewelry, electronic devices, and the latest and the greatest gadgets can stifle your wealth-building plan. A good question to ask yourself is this, how much will this item be worth in the future? More or less than you originally paid for it? I can't tell you how many items I paid top dollar for that are worth nothing today because I got caught up in trends. I met a business owner at a networking event with his logo on his tee shirt and other pieces of clothing he owned. He said he was mentored to invest in his brand, not someone else's. He saw the value of deprecation and not getting caught up in the buzz.

Be realistic about how much money you save to grow your assets. You can't overlook any debt like credit cards and student loans. Consult with a financial professional or credit specialist to devise a plan to reduce and eliminate debt. Consideration will be given to how much interest you pay on your debt compared to how much you can earn on growing your assets. We want to operate from a position of financial power by getting our arms around our entire financial picture. Don't be afraid to face debt and share this critical information with your financial professional.

The benefits of a wealth-building plan are that you will learn financial discipline that will pay off in the most critical years of your life. You can see the light at the end of the tunnel and know that you have set the time when you want to stop working for your money. By following these guidelines, you are setting up income for the future that offers you the lifestyle you have now or even better. A wealth-building plan with sound strategies will help you navigate life events and give you financial security, long-term sustainability, and peace of mind. Wealth building and wealth management can ride together. Wealth building is the beginning of wealth management. You start with a plan, acquire your assets, and then work with a financial professional to help guide you and manage your financial portfolio.

You must know your number as part of your wealth-building plan. Where do you want to be financially, and at what stage and age in your life? This complex question involves dissecting components of your life and lifestyle. Are you single? Do you plan to have a life partner, or kids, own a home, acquire higher education, establish a career, or start a business? What does your debt look like and your credit score? Is your present income sufficient to meet your wealth-building plan? If not, you may need to consider a job change or start a new career path. Some people have worked twenty, thirty, and forty years at a job only to meet living expenses without any money to save for their future life or grow assets for life beyond earning income. The financial outcome could have been different if they had set up a wealth-building plan and understood the difference between earning a paycheck and generating enough income to have a life beyond work later on in life. Have you had this discussion with your young adults to help them see the value of wealth-building early in life? This is where speaking with a financial professional can help put all these pieces together to form your personalized plan.

> **Wealth building is the beginning of wealth management.**

It's never too late to start your wealth-building plan. I started my plan several years ago, and I already see results in my financial house, I feel more financially secure knowing that I have set up income resources for my future. I walk the talk, which is why I share my life experiences to benefit others. Financial education is a great start. Some people are not sure what to expect from a financial professional. The worst question is the one you don't ask. Don't hesitate to ask for more clarity on a matter. This is your financial future, and you should understand where you are going and how you will get there. There have been times when I have had to do additional research and dig deeper so that I could help my clients understand the end goal in terms that they could understand. Your financial future is important and should be treated with the highest level of integrity.

Investing is a component of wealth building that can be the cog in the wheel for beginners when taking the leap into the world of assets under management. Noel Ramos, Registered Representative with Capital Choice Financial Group, shares some tips on investing:

Noel Ramos-

When it comes to investing, time is NOT your enemy! Too many times, we shy away from things we don't understand. That's why it is crucial to get a professional expert who will take the time to sit and educate you on what your options are. I like to start with the basic fundamentals with my clients and educate them on how they can protect their wealth and how they can make their money grow through compounding interest. Finding that right combination of good growing mutual funds is where a professional can help you.

I have found some people feel they need a lot of money to start investing, but that is not the case at all. If you want to be able to retire with dignity and change your family dynamics, come up with a game plan. It should be flexible but firm, and you have to stick to it!

CHAPTER SEVENTEEN

SOURCES OF INCOME

As we have discussed, income is at the forefront of wealth building strategies. There are some scenarios where persons have inherited sums, received a cash settlement, or hit the lottery. Even in those cases, preservation of cash and continued growth can be important to one's desired financial independence and desired lifestyle. Having a good job with good pay is only the tip of the financial iceberg. We must understand the three types of income to effectively feed our wealth building plan: Active, Passive, and Portfolio.

ACTIVE INCOME

Active Income means that we are physically engaging in actions to generate income. This list includes salaries, bonuses, wages, commissions, and consultation services. The IRS defines earned income as:

IRS TYPES OF EARNED INCOME

Wages, salary or tips where federal income taxes are withheld on Form W-2, box 1

Income from a job where your employer didn't withhold tax (such as gig economy work) including:

- ☐ Driving a car for booked rides or deliveries
- ☐ Running errands or doing tasks
- ☐ Selling goods online
- ☐ Providing creative or professional services
- ☐ Providing other temporary, on-demand or freelance work

Money made from self-employment, including if you:

- ☐ Own or operate a business or farm
- ☐ Are a minister or member of a religious order
- ☐ Are a statutory employee and have income

PASSIVE INCOME

Any rental or business activity in which an individual does not materially participate. This may include initial start-up activity.

Passive Income

- ☐ Renting equipment
- ☐ Renting real estate
- ☐ Investing In a business (You are not active in)
- ☐ Renting storage units
- ☐ Renting property space
- ☐ Licensing music
- ☐ Royalties from books
- ☐ Rent your vehicle out to someone
- ☐ Affiliate Marketing
- ☐ Dividends
- ☐ Multi-Level Marketing

PORTFOLIO INCOME

Portfolio income is known as investment income. This income class comes from interest, dividends, or capital gains. It can be derived from investments or money lent.

Portfolio Income

Snapshot of Financial Wealth

- ☐ Savings Bonds
- ☐ Limited Partnerships
- ☐ Mutual Funds
- ☐ Stock/Shares
- ☐ Insurance Policies
- ☐ Retirement Funds
- ☐ Capital Gains
- ☐ Collectibles
- ☐ Currency Exchange
- ☐ Certificates of Deposits
- ☐ Real-estate Investments
- ☐ EFT's

PORTFOLIO RETIREMENT ASSETS

Retirement assets are income strategy products. Various types of options include variable – risk and fix index – no risk. This information is for educational purposes only. Always consult with a financial and tax professional for more information.

Types Of Portfolio Retirement Assets

Traditional IRA	Roth IRA	Annuity
Individual Retirement Account	After Tax Dollars	
• Earned income directed pretax toward investments that can grow tax-deferred.	• May be withdrawn after age 59 ½ Tax Free after 5 years	• Insurance Product pays a stream of retirement income. Accrues Tax Deferred
• Can be Variable and Fixed	• Can be Variable and Fixed	• 3 Types: Fixed – Variable - Index
• SDIRA (Self Directed IRA)	• SDIRA (Self Directed IRA)	• May Provide Probate, Bankruptcy and Credit Protection

*Always Consult with a tax Advisor on Tax Strategies

Portfolio Company Sponsored Plans 401K

- Usually provided by employer, with payroll contributions
- May offer employer matching contributions
- Limited range of mutual funds and EFT's
- Employee cannot contribute once employee is severed
- Employment severed leaves two options
  - Leave Funds there without touching
  - Roll funds out to gain access to funds

INSURANCE ASSETS PORTFOLIO INCOME

There may be times in one's life when we are faced with dire health issues that require a need for a sum of money. Perhaps to pay medical bills or to save one's home from going into foreclosure due to a terminal illness that has drained income sources. Life insurance offers income protection from life events that can stop a person's income flow, such as critical, chronic, terminal illness and death. In general, a life insurance policy offers a death benefit. But what if a household is in dire need of cash while living? Besides accelerated death benefits, two options are presented based on a qualifying event.

Insurance Assets Portfolio Income

Viatical

- Investors buy the full policy or a portion of it at a cost that is less than the policy's death benefit.

- For someone who is terminally ill to obtain immediate cash they can use to pay for their care and comfort in their final days.

- Preserve their estate's other assets–such as a home–which they may not want to sell before their death.

Life Settlement

- Sale of an existing insurance policy to a third party for a one-time cash payment.

- The policy's purchaser becomes its beneficiary and assumes payment of its premiums, and receives the death benefit when the insured dies.

- Sold due to unaffordable premiums emergencies and Health Changes

- Supplements Retirement Income

MULTIFAMILY SYNDICATION INCOME

There is another type of income that could fall into Active Income, Passive Income, and Portfolio Income called Multifamily Syndication. The active partners are fully engaged in the day to operations, while passive partners reap financial passive income simply by investing with little to no other involvement. The property partnership falls into the portfolio income buck while the income could be active or passive, depending on your level of involvement. To fully understand this process, I tapped into experienced professional resources, Dr. Hoa Nguyen and Dr. Jaime Gonzalez, seasoned, full-time multifamily investors, syndicators, and asset managers. They have invested in over

6,900 units as general partners/limited partners in Texas, Arizona, Florida, and the Carolinas. Dr. Hoa and Dr. Jaime own over $480M in multifamily investments and have over 2,600 units as general partners. They also own multiple multimillion-dollar optometry practices in the Dallas area. They enjoy traveling the world for delicious food and interesting cultures in their spare time. They have a busy eight-year-old daughter Athena and a puppy named Coco Ollie.

Dr. Hoa Nguyen and Dr. Jaime Gonzalez give us a brief overview of how multifamily syndication works:[20]

Multifamily syndication is a great way for people to have their money work for them leveraging an experienced team in buying apartment communities and receiving passive income. It is truly a "done-for-you" model and apartment investing is one of the most conservative asset classes and a great way to preserve wealth and build long-term generational wealth.

The general partners actively build broker relationships for deal flow, underwrite the deals, perform the market analysis, review all contracts with the syndication attorneys, hire the property management company, perform due diligence, work with the lenders for the best debt structure, and provide these investment opportunities to limited partners to have ownership shares in the LLC of the property. The team has an asset manager who will overlook the property management company to do weekly calls, deep dive into reviewing all the monthly financial reports provided by the property management company and sends a summary of what is happening on the property with the detailed financials to all investors. Transparency and communication are integral parts of the business.

Passive investors, also known as limited partners, enjoy all of the benefits without doing any of the work, thereby creating more choices to live life on their own terms. Many people are not even aware that investment opportunities like this exist. Usually the minimum investment starts at $50,000 and the property is held for 3-5 years.

Limited partners receive all the benefits like general partners, such as cash flow, appreciation, scalability of their real estate portfolio and tax advantages with accelerated bonus depreciation which makes it a very attractive investment.

The business model is to transform and improve these communities for residents. It is a win-win model for both residents and investors.

If you are interested in learning more, you can visit www.passive wealth23.com

CHAPTER EIGHTEEN

FINANCIAL LEGACY

A financial legacy is an indelible footprint that a person leaves behind to their loved ones, estate, and charity. Empires have been handed down from generation to generation, and in other countries, royalties, kingship, and queenship are left to heirs. A financial legacy ensures that families can maintain their current lifestyle or upscale it to meet their dreams. When my father passed away, my mother was able to keep her home even though she had retired and dad was still working at the time of his death. He had a few financial items in place which gave her peace of mind and lifestyle security. Financial literacy plays a major role in building a financial legacy. Darryl Johnson, RMD Financial coach with Capital Choice Financial Group, shares his thirty-plus years of knowledge in working with clients on the subject of financial legacy below:

> Financial literacy plays a major role in building a financial legacy.

Darryl Johnson-

Financial literacy is the ability to understand and effectively use various financial skills, budgeting, and investing your money.

Financial literacy is the foundation of our relationship with money but is not a required subject in the current school system. I like to illustrate it like this: What are the chances of winning any game if you don't know the rules? Well to win the money game we need to know the rules and winning strategies. Most of us learn the financial rules by default and that impacts our children's future and the legacy we leave them.

Benefits of a Financial Legacy

- Spouse keeps the family home.

- Kids go to college or start a business.

- Debt and taxes are paid, leaving a positive financial portfolio.

There are varying views on leaving money and assets behind to loved ones, often related to cultural generations. Some famous people left nothing at all and some left an abundance. An article published in Newsweek on March 3rd, 2019, reported that Michael Jackson allegedly was broke at the time of his death and was between $400 million and $500 million in debt. Since then, the King of Pop has earned significant royalties from his work that continues to be sold.[21] Sammy Davis Jr died with a $5.2million dollar debt to the IRS, according to celebritynetworth.com.[22] The article states that his $4 million estate wasn't enough to cover his tax debts, forcing his widow to auction off his possessions. Who enjoys an M&M and a Mar's candy bar? Forrest Mars was the recipient of his father Frank Mars' estate when Frank passed in 1934, according to therichest.com/lifestyles. The Mars estate is worth billions.[23] Have you given thought to your family's financial future?

NET WORTH

Have you ever been asked what your net worth was and did not have a clue? Don't be alarmed, as quite a few people don't know or understand their net worth and how to calculate it. Net worth is assets minus liabilities (debt), which equals a monetary value that could be negative or positive. Let's review just a few categories:

Assets comprise of checking and savings accounts, currency exchange, EFTs, retirement savings, automobiles, boats, real estate, collectibles, certificates of deposit, and other cash-positive value items.

Liabilities include all debt, such as IRS balances, credit cards, student loans, mortgages, auto loans, bank loans, and other debt.

Every household should know their net worth, single, married, or significant other. This means we must be aware of our assets and liabilities. I have seen relationships where the wife or husband did not know their family's financial status, including total debt, income, and assets, and therefore couldn't make any determination of their net worth.

Estate Planning is another component used to protect and channel your net worth beyond a person's lifespan. Attorney at Law, Dina Arvanitakis, specializes in Estate Planning, Real Estate and Probate and explains the value of implementing an estate plan:

> *When you don't have an estate plan in place, you can inadvertently create an expensive nightmare for the loved ones left behind. Whether you die with a will or not, all of your assets that are solely in your name are frozen and will have to go through probate. Probate is a court-supervised process where the executor marshals all the assets determines your creditors, pays them and, if there is anything left over, any remaining assets go to the beneficiaries. If you want to avoid the probate process, you need more than just a will. You need to set up a trust and designate beneficiaries in advance of your death so that your assets can pass without the need to probate your estate. Alternatively, if the only asset you have is your home, in the state of Florida, you can do a Lady Bird deed whereby the house can pass to your children upon your death without the need for a probate. This powerful probate avoidance deed is available only in the state of Florida, Michigan, Texas, Vermont and West Virginia.*

Another benefit for having an estate plan in place is it protects your children, especially if they are still minors. You can designate a pre-need guardian for them in case both parents pass away before they reach the age of majority. When you fail to plan, you are planning to fail. Planning ahead saves time, money and stress.[24]

A last will (Will) ensures that "Thy will is done." Retaining power over one's estate requires understanding the purpose and value of having an executable will or trust upon one's death, as mentioned above. The artist Prince died without a will, and after months of legal battles, his sister and five-half siblings became heirs to his multi-million-dollar estate, according to an article in USA Today on August 22nd, 2018.[25] I was married for over twenty years and never had a will in place. No one ever talked to me about a will, but I think, in part, I did not think I was worthy of having a will in place. In my mind, wills were for the rich and famous people. That mindset couldn't be further from the truth if you have money in the bank, a home, children, heirlooms, collectibles, real estate, a business, and other assets, you need to have a will. There are endless do-it-yourself will kits on the market, and if you choose this option, take the extra step to secure the signatures of witnesses. A will can be prepared by an attorney, who is a great option to ensure legal enforceability, unlike a trust which a legal professional must prepare. When my grandmother passed away, she left behind her family home. The home went into probate, and all surviving relatives had to sign off on the home to go to one relative. The drill down on biological relatives went down to half-siblings who had to be located. Everyone agreed on who would get the property without any issues. This is not always the case. Sometimes there are major disputes that can last months and years. Always consult with an attorney for the laws in your state.

> When you fail to plan, you are planning to fail.

Life Insurance is another instrument that can be used to leave a financial legacy and can be listed in a trust if you so desire. Often, people look at life insurance as burial money. Under consideration is the life and livelihood for our loved ones should we fall away in death. Have we taken the necessary steps to ensure that the ones we love and care about have the same or better manner of living once we are gone? The question of life insurance always comes up after a person dies, but why not before? As mentioned earlier, think ahead, past our life, have we given thought to retain the home our family resides in, higher education, or a business for our children and funding daily living expenses for years? There is a process for determining how much life insurance a person would need to set up a financial legacy that leaves our loved ones feeling safe and secure for the lifestyle that you desire them to have. We will discuss more on life insurance as a component of financial security.

A financial legacy can be viewed as a person's inheritance. An inheritance (a component in a will and trust) is nothing more than handing over one's assets after death. This includes cars, cash, bank accounts, jewelry, collectibles, and other financial portfolio assets. The term inheritance relates immediately to wealth and assets over the word will, trust, probate, and life insurance. All of these terms connect to the surviving family receiving assets. Consider the laws in your state regarding leaving an inheritance to minor children. Always consult with a legal professional before making any decisions.

CHAPTER NINETEEN

FINANCIAL SECURITY

Financial security is knowing that you are prepared for events that can impact you now and in years to come, planned and unplanned. Think of a home with a security system that would cover all entry points, not just a select few. Shoring up your financial house will give you added security and peace of mind knowing you have covered all bases and have not left any financial entry point open. We will discuss a few focus areas, however, more may be needed depending on your customized financial game plan.

Life insurance is one of the most critical elements of financial security that seems complex to some and undervalued by others. Life insurance offers income protection beyond burial costs. The face value of the policy should be considerate of funeral costs and survivorship income funds for family members, such as a spouse or children. Insurance policies may also add another layer of financial security by listing the mortgage holder as a beneficiary. A word on the types of mortgage-related insurance:

> Life insurance is one of the most critical elements of financial security.

Protecting the Lender

To protect the lender if you stop making payments, Private Mortgage Insurance (PMI) may be required as part of the home closing process.

Protecting the Borrower/Heirs - YOU

Mortgage Title Insurance protects the heirs in case the title is not free and clear at the time of the home purchase.

Mortgage Protection Life Insurance

Protects the borrower and their heirs depending on what type of policy is purchased. The lender may be listed as a beneficiary. Consult with a licensed insurance agent for more details and clarification.

History reveals to us the opportunities to attain life insurance that was not available in the past. In the late 1800s, women were not allowed to be insured with life insurance until the efforts of Bina M. West. Miss West, a twenty-four-year-old schoolteacher, witnessed the demise of two of her students when their mother passed away, leaving the father with little financial means to care for them. According to an article in Historyswomen.com/socialreformer, the father placed the children in separate foster homes. Later the girl would be hired as a domestic servant, and the boy would work in a stable. Miss West would be instrumental in providing life insurance to women. There was also a time when it was illegal for a wife to take out life insurance on herself or her husband. The husband could take out a life insurance policy on his own life and name his wife or children as beneficiaries. However, because the policy was considered part of his estate, creditors had access to the funds, which could leave the wife and children financially distressed and, in some cases, broke and homeless.[26]

We are happy that we have come a long way in opening up household rights for financial security. In today's times, life insurance is readily available to all genders and ages in consideration of one's medical history and risk factors. Care should be given to understanding the types of life insurance and what is best for a person's individual and household needs. There are two basic Death Benefit life insurance types: Term and Permanent.

TERM LIFE INSURANCE

All Term Life Insurance offers a death benefit, and some will offer an accelerated death benefit, or what can be referred to as Living Benefits, through a specific period or term. Death benefit means that when a person dies, the face value of the policy becomes the death benefit paid out to the beneficiary or beneficiaries. Level Term means that the monthly premium will never change during the policy term period. Renewable term means that the policy can be renewed at the end of the initial term of years at rates based on the insured age and current medical conditions. Yearly Renewable means that the policy is renewable each year, there is no set period, and the premiums are subject to one's age and health condition at the time of renewal. Decreasing term means the policy's death benefit decreases yearly, while the premium remains level. Some term policies can go up to around the age of 100, again subject to age and health conditions. Consult with a financial professional for more detail. Living Benefits or accelerated death benefits offer the insured access to a percentage of the face value of the policy while living by filing a medical claim with the respective carrier. These claims are evaluated based on health triggers covered by the insurance carrier and can offer a cash payout to the insured while living. A cash payout will reduce the face value of the policy. This payout is not a loan. In general, Term Life insurance premiums are lower than permanent premiums. Consult with a qualified insurance agent and tax professional for more detail and to review the type of policy that is right for you.

PERMANENT LIFE INSURANCE

Permanent Life Insurance does not have a set number of years and is considered to cover one's lifetime. There are two basic types, Whole Life and Universal Life Insurance. Both types offer a death benefit and a cash value savings element. The cash value can be available to borrow with interest. The face value will be reduced by the loan if not paid back in full. Universal Life's cash value is based on the market performance, and the premiums are structured differently from Whole Life. There may be some tax considerations that could be advantageous with some permanent insurance policies. Permanent Life Insurance premiums are higher than term because of combing the death benefit with a cash value component. The rules of a Whole Life Policy are that the cash value is not paid out to the beneficiary upon insured's death and the death benefit can be canceled if all the cash value is withdrawn prior to the insured's death. Consult with a qualified insurance agent and tax professional for more detail and to review the type of policy that is right for you.

RETIREMENT INCOME

Retirement means we are disconnecting from generating active income. We are no longer concerned with punching a time clock, reporting to work, logging into a computer by a certain time, meeting deadlines, and trying to balance work with personal life. If we have done this right, we are prepared financially to have the lifestyle we desire and complete time freedom without worrying about income. We have discussed the need for a financial game plan, and by doing this earlier, you are now prepared to unplug and enjoy life to the fullest, whatever that means for you. Below we will discuss a few retirement options that have already been referred to in this book.

ANNUITIES

An annuity is an insurance product that offers various future income disbursements over time or immediately upon funding according to contract rules. This steady income stream makes an annuity appealing, along with tax deferment. Annuities are not related to life insurance. Annuities may not become subject to probate and some creditors.

You must consult a licensed insurance agent and attorney in your state pertaining to the locale.

Fixed Indexed: You will never lose your principle and you retain your gain. There is no risk with this type of product. Consult with a tax professional and insurance agent for more details and clarification.

Variable: The principle is at risk. There is the potential for higher gain and greater loss. There are options for risk tolerance. This is for educational purposes only. Consult with a securities licensed and tax professional for more detail and clarification.

IRA

An IRA (Individual Retirement Account) is an account funded with earned income for long-term savings with tax advantages (Consult with a tax professional). There are various types of IRAs, including Traditional IRAs, Roth IRAs, SIMPLE (Savings Incentive Employee Match Plans), and SEP (Simplified Employee Pension) IRAs. Some of these product types can be fixed (no risk) or variable (risk). Check with your life insurance agent, tax professional, and securities licensed professional for more details, clarification, and insight on income rules, taxation, and withdrawals. The goal is long-term retirement savings.

401K

A 401k plan is a long-term retirement savings account in which the employee, through a payroll deduction, is contributing pre-tax dollars. Some employees may offer a percentage of matching contributions. I call this free money. The employee usually has a variety of investment options. Check with your employer for plan rules on the percentage of contributions and withdrawal plan rules.

IDENTITY PROTECTION

Once you have established your financial footprint, consider taking appropriate measures to protect your valuable assets. Financial security includes protecting your identity, data, and sensitive information. Whitney Hartford, an independent representative with Reliashield, shares her personal experience with identity theft:

> **Whitney Hartford-**
>
> *https://identitytheft.org/statistics/ states that in 2021, there were 5.7 million reports of identity theft and fraud. Everything we access or utilize is online. We need to be more diligent with protecting our personal information. As a victim of identity theft myself I will tell you it's not something I would wish upon anyone. The amount of time it took me to contact the credit bureaus to dispute false charges, the level of stress and anxiety added to my life at the time wasn't worth the headache. Had I been proactive and frozen my credit or invested in a super affordable identity theft protection plan and had a company monitor the activity associated with my personal information I would have saved myself the headache. I highly recommend getting an identity theft protection plan or freezing your credit. Either one will give you the peace of mind that your credit is protected and you have the ability to temporarily unfreeze your credit when needed.* [27]

Our financial game plan includes a wealth-building plan and retirement strategy. We have learned the value of protecting our nest eggs, and now we need to determine who needs to know about it and where to locate our documents for safekeeping.

CHAPTER TWENTY

WHO NEEDS TO KNOW

The first person that needs to know their financial status and position is you. The first step to harnessing and growing your assets is to know your financial position. Financial data tracking is a great way to have a bird's eye view of your money flow. I sat down with Austin Farmer, a data analyst, to get his recommendations on a best practice for financial tracking. He shares his tips below:

Austin Farmer -

As the old saying goes, what is not tracked can't be improved (Peter Drucker). In order to chart your path toward financial freedom you need to understand your current financial position in detail and must keep a close eye on it along your journey. Ideally, the process of continuously tracking your financial position should begin long before you have even established a financial goal. In short, tracking your financial position is the exercise of documenting how money, assets and debt are flowing in and out of your possession. Use a data tool like Excel or Google Sheets to begin tracking your financial position and start with these 4 categories: Monthly Net Income, Monthly Expenses, Total Savings/Investments, and Total Debt. Within your Monthly Net Income bucket, list the after-tax amount of each stream of income you have coming to you. Break your Monthly Expenses category into two buckets, Variable and Fixed expenses. Each and every expense should be accounted for in this section. Variable expenses are expenses that change month over month so put an average for each one, be sure to round up! Your fixed expenses are expenses that are the same each month like your rent or mortgage. In the Savings/Investments category, break out the total amount of money you have in your checking and savings accounts, the total amount of money you have invested as well as any equity you have in your assets. Finally, your Debt category should be a breakdown of your total debt by each debtor. Once you have completed this exercise, total up each section and review how much money you have in each category. What you see now is your current financial position. Now, you can get started on creating a path toward your financial goal. And don't forget, this exercise should be done on a consistent basis. Every 6 months or as income, expenses or debt significantly change. Stay in tune with your financial position to stay on track toward achieving your financial goal.

What you don't know can hurt you, especially in tax strategies and your financial obligations bound by the law. Have you heard this said, "Hire your weakness?" Consulting with a seasoned tax professional can help save you from costly financial mistakes. It's always in your best interest to be proactive and consult with a tax professional rather than being reactive to putting out a tax burden fire. Deidra Pittman, CEO of Tax Deivas, has been in the tax business for decades and shares her insight into the value advance client tax consultations:

> **What you don't know can hurt you, especially in tax strategies and your financial obligations bound by the law.**

Deidra Pittman-

I used to think that if a person is old enough to work a job and have federal withholdings taken out, they need to understand their taxes and financial obligations. In the last ten years, I have changed my mind. I am now convinced that educating, informing, and guiding needs to start at a very early age like elementary school. Yes, they are not too young to be taught finances and taxes on their level. I call it preventative measures.

Ignorance is definitely not bliss and especially when it comes to your taxes and business. One real story sticks in my mind. I had a client who decided he would file his corporation with the Secretary of State, and he did. Not knowing the filing would only secure his business entity but had nothing to do with how he wanted his corporation taxed. The client unknowingly filed as a corporation and at tax time he got hit hard. If he had known to file, the corporation with the Secretary of State then once it was approved to file Form 2553 with the IRS to elect for his corporation to be taxed as an S Corp he would not have owed the IRS $40,000. Yes, that little bit of ignorance cost him thousands of dollars.

Financial conversations are extremely important in relationships, whether persons are living under the same roof or contemplating starting a household together. Building a financial house starts with a foundation that includes knowledge, viewpoints, and short and long-term financial goals.

I had conversations with some twenty-something males and females, and they have expressed frustration when attempting to bring up the topic of finances with their romantic interest. They say it feels awkward. Why would that be? One reason is that we are not talking about money goals enough with our up-and-coming generations. Schools are not teaching money talk. As a financial coach, I recommend having a financial conversation with potential serious partners on their views of debt, spending, savings and investments, wealth building, and sources of income. What I do hear from young people to mature adults is bragging rights on income and careers. We are teaching our young people to get jobs with good pay, maybe settle down one day, purchase a home, and start a family. Who is teaching them to build a financial house? Let's break the generational curse by having conversations with our kids, including landing a job, creating passive income, and building a financial portfolio that includes retirement security. Sad to say, I am just having these conversations with my children, but it's never too late, and they are listening and making changes. I encourage dating couples, husbands, wives, and significant others to have that conversation, not one time but ongoing. Again, all too often, wives will tell me their husbands handle all the finances and that they can't answer some basic questions about their family's financial house. A financial house is constructed to protect human and tangible assets with various insurances, eliminate debt, saving for emergencies, setting up for retirement, investments, growth and income strategies (wealth building), college or entrepreneurial pursuits, and charity.

Establish a safe place for legal and financial documents in which you have entrusted an entity or institution or entrust its location to a person or persons. These documents include your last will, Life Insurance Policies, Retirement and Investment products, financial accounts, heirlooms, and any estate-related paperwork needed to carry out your wishes. I recall years ago, a presumed financially well-to-do businessman who unexpectedly passed away, leaving a wife and adult children behind. To this day, no one has found his financial assets. The family remains devastated, and the wife is left penniless other than what she can earn on her own for survival. We can avoid these tragic situations by communicating with our family in advance. If you keep a safe in your home, ensure that only trusted persons have access or combinations. Should you choose a bank safety deposit box, ensure that someone has a key and knows the box number. You can make a copy of your last will, but someone will need to produce the original for legal validation.

> Establish a safe place for legal and financial documents.

Consider age-appropriate information when sharing financial information with minor children and even teens. Discussing financially sensitive information can be overwhelming for young minds, and there is the issue of maintaining confidentiality. Also, peers can influence the brightest kids into mischief with family assets.

Protect your financial house by not inviting the wrong people inside that will take advantage of you. You could unknowingly invite persons into your life that have bad intentions to deplete you of your assets. Sad to say, sharing your financial assets with friends and some family may not be wise. Generalities are one thing but avoid discussing and sharing specifics like bank balances, cash, jewelry, heirlooms, passwords, financial institution account names, and numbers.

We have unlocked the strategy for wealth building and the simple steps to securing a financial future. We began by tapping into various income sources, including active income, passive income, and portfolio income. Start building a financial legacy for your loved ones so that they will have an adequate lifestyle. Set up a foundation of financial security, including income protection and retirement. Ensure that you are well educated and informed on your financial picture and take the proper measures to protect your financial house. Always consult with a tax professional, estate planner, attorney, and licensed insurance agent. This information is for educational purposes and is not intended to offer advisement.

CHAPTER TWENTY-ONE

FINANCIAL FREEDOM

The status of financial freedom or independence can be seemingly elusive for our mass global human population. My definition of financial freedom is complete ownership of one's time and resources as outlined below:

- Financial Freedom - the ability to seize opportunities.

- The freedom to travel at a moment's notice.

- The mental clarity to author books at any time.

- The availability to support community efforts to enrich and build.

- To help build strong networks of collaborations.

- To mentor and coach others within one's skillset.

Some people see financial freedom as an over-abundance of money complete with lavish living. A business acquaintance found financial freedom when she gave up her six-figure career job and donated years of her life to helping underprivileged children without any income compensation.

Dr. Shellie Hipsky, CEO of Inspiring Lives International, the Executive Director of the Global Sisterhood (which helps women and children around the world), and the editor-in-chief of Inspiring Lives Magazine shares her perspective on financial freedom:

Dr. Shellie Hipsky-

Financial freedom is the power to spend and save money on one's own terms and without stress and turmoil. For me, being financially free means booking a family vacation on a whim so that I can enjoy bonding time with my kids. It means having my house and cars paid off, living debt-free and happy. It means being able to invest and give to charities when my heart leads me in that direction. As the Global Empowerment Coach, I lead my EmpowerU Master Class students and my World Class VIP coaching clients towards their own abundance and financial freedom through activating their action plans, determining what they truly desire, and manifesting their dreams to come true. Financial freedom is the cornerstone of inner peace when looking at yourself holistically. When one is secure and stable in one's finances and wealth creation and sustainability, they can reach new levels of success!

This book offers a blueprint for developing a healthy, informed money mindset that can put you on your way to financial freedom. How do you interpret financial freedom? For some people, there are levels of financial freedom as stated in Forbes's article *8 Levels Of Financial Freedom (forbes.com)*:[28]

Not Living Paycheck to Paycheck

Enough Money to Quit your Job (for a bit)

Enough to be Financially Happy and still Save

Freedom of Time

Enough for a Basic Retirement

Enough to Actually Retire Well

Enough for Dream Retirement

More Money Than You Could Ever Spend

Attaining financial freedom is the result of financial game planning at the earliest stages of one's life. We have seen families inherit financial freedom money and lose it, while others multiplied and grew their financial legacy. Lottery winners became wealthy overnight and broke over time. Financial freedom is not always wealth. Ask the man or woman that you see on the fishing piers without a care in their world. No debt, low living expenses, and living free of financial burdens. No matter how you slice it, this still comes down to properly managing one's finances.

> Financial freedom is not always wealth.

CHAPTER TWENTY-TWO

CONCLUSION

We live in a world where the currency is the lifeblood across all continents. Our existence of survival, including food, water, clothing, and shelter, is determined by the abundance or lack of money. Intentional money is fluid, in motion, moving, growing, and multiplying for the present, future, and family generations to come. Think about the vibe we transmit to others when handling money. There is an old saying, *Esse quam videri*, which means "To Be Rather Than to Seem." The world is full of pictures and movies of inflated wealth and successes that are not real. There is nothing wrong with living within our financial ability and the lifestyle we desire. Start by reading books, and consulting with licensed financial professionals, mentors, and coaches. Commit to learn and be coachable. The time to start building your financial house is now.

"Work hard for your money and then plan for your money to work for you."

ENDNOTES

1   "7 Currencies Worth More than the Dollar" - https://www.investopedia.com/articles/forex/030216/6-strongest-currencies-vs-us-dollar-2016.asp

2   "10 Countries Where the U.S. Dollar Goes the Furthest" - https://financebuzz.com/countries-where-dollar-goes-furthest

3   Los Angeles Herald, Volume 44, Number 82, 2 July 1895 - https://cdnc.ucr.edu/cgi-bin/cdnc?a=d&d=LAH18950702.2.38.4

4   Merriam Webster Dictionary - https://www.merriam-webster.com/dictionary/loan#:~:text=%3A%20something%20lent%20usually%20for%20the,the%20grant%20of%20temporary%20use

5   Cosign - https://www.investopedia.com/terms/c/co_sign.asp

6   Oxford Dictionary - https://www.oxfordlearnersdictionaries.com/us/definition/american_english/philanthropy

7   Katrina Impacts - http://www.hurricanescience.org/history/studies/katrinacase/impacts/

8   Estate Planning Tip: Be Aware of a Recent Court Ruling that "Loan" is Actually a Gift - https://www.millermillercanby.com/

estate-planning-tip-be-aware-of-a-recent-tax-court-ruling-that-loan-is-actually-a-gift/

9   7 Tax Rules to Know if You Give or Receive Cash - https://money.usnews.com/money/personal-finance/taxes/articles/gift-tax-tax-rules-to-know-if-you-give-or-receive-cash#:~:text=You%20Don't%20Have%20to,to%20pay%20a%20gift%20tax.

10 https://www.moneysmartguides.com/

11 Why is American Currency Green? - https://www.history.com/news/why-is-american-currency-green

12 Your Change Makes the TSA Wealthier - https://zh-cn.facebook.com/VWGWealthManagement/posts/fun-fact-fridayyour-change-makes-the-tsa-wealthier-change-adds-up-fast-in-2015-t/2472013012898196/

13   https://www.prenuptialagreements.org/

14 Why is American Currency Green? - https://www.history.com/news/why-is-american-currency-green

15 Gilbert, D. (2002) The American Class Structure: In An Age of Growing Inequality. Belmont, CA: Wadsworth, ISBN 0534541100. (see also Gilbert Model); Thompson, W. & Hickey, J. (2005). Society in Focus. Boston, MA: Pearson, Allyn & Bacon; Beeghley, L. (2004). The Structure of Social Stratification in the United States. Boston, MA: Pearson, Allyn & Bacon.

16 The Richest People in the World (Who Look Like They're Poor) - https://www.therichest.com/high-life/15-of-the-richest-people-in-the-world-who-look-like-theyre-poor/

17 Steve Benson Mother and Brother in Florida Bomb Attack - https://www.oxygen.com/florida-man-murders/crime-news/steven-benson-murdered-mother-brother-in-florida-bomb-attack

18 10 Most Expensive Divorce Settlements in History - https://manofmany.com/lifestyle/most-expensive-divorce-settlements-in-history

19 Merriam Webster Dictionary - https://www.merriam-webster.com/dictionary/wealth

20 www.passivewealth23.com

21 https://www.newsweek.com/topic/michael-jackson?page=2

22 Sammy Davis Jr. Net Worth - https://www.celebritynetworth.com/richest-celebrities/singers/sammy-davis-jr-net-worth/

23 These Are the Richest Members of the Mars Family and a Peek at Their Lavish Lifestyle - https://www.therichest.com/rich-powerful/these-are-the-richest-members-of-the-mars-family-and-a-peek-at-their-lavish-lifestyle/

24 Dina Arvanitakis - https://alg-legal.com/about/

25 https://www.usatoday.com/sitemap/2017/august/22/

26 From Coverture to Contract: Engendering Insurance on Lives (yale.edu).

27 https://identitytheft.org/statistics/

28 8 Levels Of Financial Freedom (forbes.com)

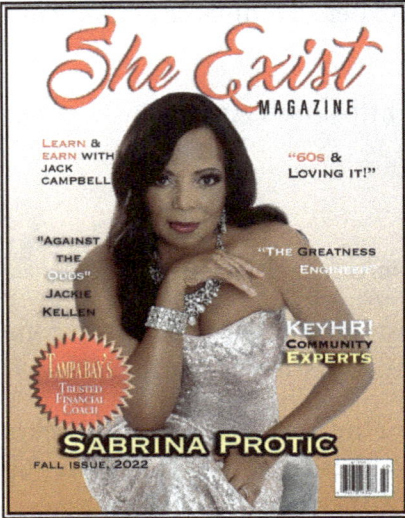

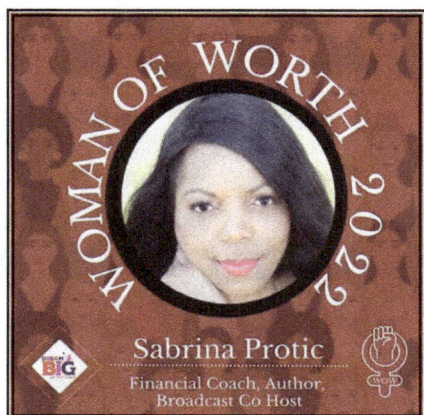

WOMAN OF WORTH 2022

Sabrina Protic

Financial Coach, Author,
Broadcast Co Host

FINANCIAL COACH
Sabrina Protic

Sabrina Protic

The UnstopABLE Stories Show with host

"UnstopABLE people with UnstopABLE stories"

TERRANCE LEFTRIDGE

Tuesday June 8, 2022 1 pm EST
Show Guests: Sabrina Protic
Show Topic: Growing Agelessly Financially
https://bit.ly/unstoppablestories

OPEN BxRx Monday I Financial Planning: "Hindsight to Insight"

THE SUCCESSFUL Woman's MINDSET

TV Show

Watch Now at: www.everydaywomantv.com

Growing your Assets

Sabrina Protic
Financial Coach
Guest

Galit Ventura - Rozen
TV - Host

Mireille Toulekima
Global Leadership
ENGINEER
Talk
SHOW
Friday June 10th 2022 @ 9.30am EDT
Topic: Growing Ageless Financially
Sabrina Protic
Financial Coach, Certified life coach, Author, Talk show co-host
MIREILLE TOULEKIMA
YOUR HOST
STEM
She Exist
WEDO
LIVE
YouTube
Linked in
THE GREATNESS ENGINEERING HOUR
https://www.youtube.com/c/MireilleToulekima

The Remedy to Losing Money and Your Power
Sabrina Protic
Financial Coach
Excerpt from Wellness for Winners
www.wellnessforwinners.com
WELLNESS FOR WINNERS
Your Guide to WELLNESS, SUCCESS and HAPPINESS
SHERRI LEOPOLD EVAN TYRO
AMAZON #1 BESTSELLER
I began to design my financial future to protect my well-being and at the same time help others.
-Sabrina Protic

"Master Leadership in Pushing UP People"
Sabrina Protic
The Book I Read Contributor
THE BOOK I READ
Best Seller
amazon.com
GET YOUR COPY TODAY!
www.TheBookIReadBook.com

NOEL RAMOS
Regional Marketing Director

CAPITAL™
CHOICE

We should all have the right to
choose our own financial path!

407-414-8461

www.capitalchoice.com

DR HOA NGUYEN &
DR JAIME GONZALEZ

BLACKSTEEL
INVESTMENT GROUP

INVEST TO
IMPACT

blacksteel Invt Grp
blacksteelinvestmentgroup
www.passivewealth23.com

DINA ARVANITAKIS

ARVANITAKIS LAW GROUP

Putting the EASE in legalese

Dina Arvanitakis, Esq.

📞 **727-600-5858**

✉ dina@alg-legal.com

🌐 www.alg-legal.com

📍 2454 N. McMullen Booth Rd. Suite 700
Clearwater, FL 33759

Real Estate, Estate Planning, Probate,
Business, Trademarks & Mediation Services

Putting the EASE in Legalese ℠

Arvanitakis Law Group, LLC
2454 N. McMullen Booth Rd., Suite 700
Clearwater, FL 33759

https://alg-legal.com/

DARRYL JOHNSON

Npartners@yahoo.com

https://thrivingwomennetwork.com

WHITNEY HARTFORD

Identity Theft Protection Agent
Small Business Website & Social Media Services
Fitness Recovery for Moms

If you feel better, you do better. If you do better, you feel better. This doesn't have to feel like a vicious cycle, if you make implementing daily good habits a lifestyle.

www.momminitlikeaboss.com

Momminitlikeaboss19@gmail.com

Improveyourlifelv@gmail.com

DEIDRA PITTMAN

TAX Deivas

PREPARATION · TRAINING · CONSULTING

We Keep It Legal, Ethical, and Compliant

---

www.taxdeivas.com

deidra@taxdeivas.com

AUSTIN FARMER

Never stop growing

DR SHELLIE HIPSKY
CEO Inspiring Lives International

INSPIRING LIVES

INTERNATIONAL

Inspiring Lives International is a motivational media company led by Dr. Shellie Hipsky that provides resources, coaching, keynotes, literature, curricula, and platforms for uplifting women around the world. The core values which have been committed to for over a decade include: empowering and inspiring the women of the world through empathy, shared experiences, knowledge, communication, and collaboration.

Inspiration is just a Story Away!

www.ShellieHipsky.com

SHE EXIST MAGAZINE

Janelle Harris CEO

SHE EXIST MAGAZINE is not just any magazine.
SHE EXIST Magazine is a luxury magazine for Women,
by Women. SHE EXIST MAGAZINE hopes to help
readers build a stronger sense of self-worth.

SABRINA PROTIC

Financial Coach
World Class Partners Associates

Sabrina
LIFE & FINANCIAL COACH

The decisions we make today will
impact our financial tomorrow.

813-400-3019

www.sabrinaprotic.com

#HindsightToInsight

NOW Publishing Presents

SABRINA PROTIC'S
SIGNATURE BOOKS

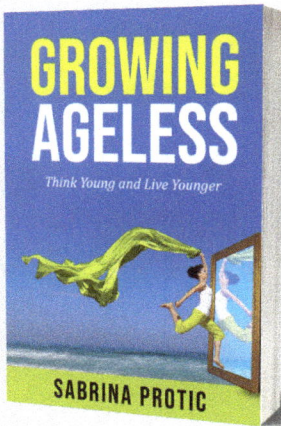

Growing Ageless:

Think Young and
Live Younger

**Hindsight
To Insight:**

Money Between
Family & Friends

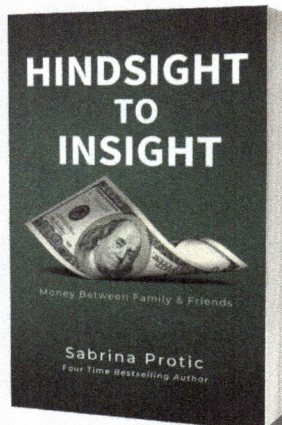

Do You Want to Make an Impact?

NOW Publishing will help you build your book and deliver your message in a powerful, impactful way.

Everyone has a story to tell and NOW Publishing is here to help them bring those stories to life. Whether you have already written a book and need a marketing partner to promote your story, or have an idea for a book that can change lives and inspire others, we are here to help you turn that into something memorable and marketable.

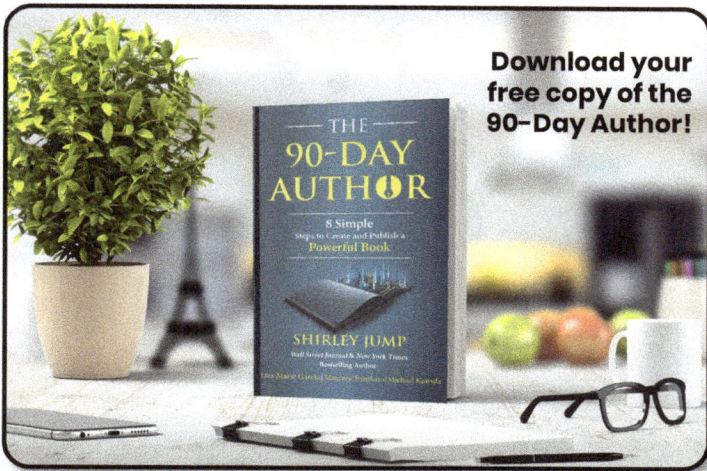

Download your free copy of the 90-Day Author!

THE 90-DAY AUTHOR

8 Simple Steps to Create and Publish a Powerful Book

SHIRLEY JUMP

EMAIL US!
publish@nowscpress.com

Ask about our
90-Day Idea-to-Author Program!

NOW
PUBLISHING

VISIT US!
www.PublishWithNOW.com

ABOUT THE AUTHOR

Sabrina Protic is an international inspirational community connector and relationship builder. She is an author, motivational speaker, wife, mother, and grandmother who loves educating and empowering her community as a licensed world-class financial coach and certified life coach.

Sabrina is the author of *Growing Ageless: Think Young-Live Younger*. She's collaboratively authored *Top 25 Change Makers, Keep Smiling Dose of Hope,* and International Bestseller of *Wellness for Winners* and *The Book I Read*. She's also the COO and co-host of international streaming live *Thriving Women Talk* on E360TV. Sabrina is a featured cover girl as a trusted financial coach for *She Exist Magazine's* 2022 fall edition.

Living by the motto "Happiness is the prescription for longevity," Sabrina enjoys inspiring people to overcome obstacles and live their best lives.

Sabrina found her purpose after pivoting from the corporate world due to pandemic cutbacks. Her passion as a financial coach is to help households put financial game plans in place that pass the test of time and circumstances. Sabrina has a strong focus on educating people about establishing financial legacies and creating safe layers of financial protection and growth. Being a financial coach is a people-to-people culture. She has always loved connecting with people and lending herself to help others.

W.E.E. is an organization striving for continuous opportunities for women to expand their networks, develop relationships and grow their businesses. W.E.E. is active within the community by organizing events for women entrepreneurs and donating to various community charities each year.

Sabrina is the co-founder of *The Sharper Woman Newsletter*, a resource to help women live longer, younger, stronger and smarter lives utilizing the power of information. The sharper woman recognizes the value of information in mindfulness, mental well-being, fitness, women's bodies and financial education in preparation for events that impact her life now and in the years to come. She is equipped and informed to make smarter choices for herself and her family.

Learn more about Sabrina at www.SabrinaProtic.com

https://www.amazon.com/author/sabrinaprotic

CONNECT WITH THE AUTHOR

facebook.com/sabrina.farmer.3551

facebook.com/SabrinaProticFinancialCoach

linkedin.com/in/sabrina-farmer-protic-b7b97868/

instagram.com/discoverageless/

instagram.com/sabrinaprotic/

tiktok.com/@worldclasspartners

twitter.com/ProticSabrina

www.ingramcontent.com/pod-product-compliance
Lightning Source LLC
Chambersburg PA
CBHW071642210326
41597CB00017B/2078